the world for curious kids

countries of the world

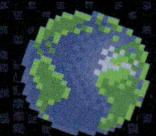
Pixelorama

the world for curious kids

Also available:

Be curious.

Before we go:

Welcome! Get ready to embark on an extraordinary journey across the globe. This unique illustrated book is designed just for you, the curious and adventurous, eager to explore every corner of our fascinating world.

Exploring the World, One Page at a Time
We've meticulously organized this book in alphabetical order, making it easy and fun to navigate. Each page is dedicated to a different country or territory, complete with its name, flag, population, and size. But that's not all – we've also included a handy mini-map for each location, so you know exactly where in the world you are! You'll also find a color code on top of each page: Red for America, Brown for Africa, Green for Europe, Orange for Asia and Purple for Oceania and the Pacific.

Fun Facts and Fascinating Details
Every page is packed with interesting and amusing facts about each place. Did you know that there's a country where you can pay with rocks? Or an island where the trees act as road signs? These are just some of the fun things you'll discover as you flip through the pages.

Retro Style, Modern Learning
The highlight of each page is the detailed, colorful pixel art illustration that captures the essence of each country or territory. These illustrations are not just fun to look at; they're a window into the diverse cultures, landscapes, and histories of our world, all in a style that echoes the charm of classic video games.

A Series for the Eager Minds
This book is part of a book series, "The World for Curious Kids." Our aim is to present the world to inquisitive minds in a way that's not just educational, but also entertaining and visually captivating. We believe that learning about our world should be an adventure, filled with awe and wonder.

Join Us on This Global Exploration
So, dear readers, are you ready to explore the world? Grab your imaginary passport, and let's start this incredible journey. Each page is a new discovery, a new adventure, and a step closer to becoming a true global citizen. Welcome to "The World for Curious Kids" – your ticket to exploring the world in a way you've never seen before!

Where are we going to ?

Red for America, Brown for Africa, Green for Europe, Orange for Asia, Purple for Oceania and the Pacific.

09 • Afghanistan
10 • Albania
11 • Algeria
12 • American Samoa (USA)
13 • Andorra
14 • Angola
15 • Anguilla (UK)
16 • Antarctica
17 • Antigua and Barbuda
18 • Argentina
19 • Armenia
20 • Aruba (Netherlands)
21 • Australia
22 • Austria
23 • Azerbaijan
23 • Azores (Portugal)
25 • Bahamas
26 • Bahrain
27 • Bangladesh
28 • Barbados
29 • Belarus
30 • Belgium
31 • Belize
32 • Benin
33 • Bermuda (UK)
34 • Bhutan
35 • Bolivia
36 • Bonaire (Netherlands)
37 • Bosnia and Herzegovina
38 • Botswana
39 • Brazil
40 • British Virgin Islands (UK)
41 • Brunei
42 • Bulgaria
43 • Burkina Faso
44 • Burundi
45 • Cabo Verde
46 • Cambodia
47 • Cameroon
48 • Canada
49 • Canary Islands (Spain)
50 • Cayman Islands (UK)
51 • Central African Republic

52 • Chad
53 • Chile
54 • China
55 • Colombia
56 • Comoros
57 • Congo-Brazzaville
58 • Cook Islands
59 • Costa Rica
60 • Côte d'Ivoire (Ivory Coast)
61 • Croatia
62 • Cuba
63 • Curaçao (Netherlands)
64 • Cyprus
65 • Czechia (Czech Republic)
66 • Democratic Republic of the Congo
67 • Denmark
68 • Djibouti
69 • Dominica
70 • Dominican Republic
71 • Ecuador
72 • Egypt
73 • El Salvador
74 • England (UK)
75 • Equatorial Guinea
76 • Eritrea
77 • Estonia
78 • Eswatini
79 • Ethiopia
80 • Falkland Islands
81 • Faroe Islands (Denmark)
82 • Fiji
83 • Finland
84 • France
85 • French Guiana (France)
86 • French Polynesia (France)
87 • Gabon
88 • Gambia
89 • Georgia
90 • Germany
91 • Ghana
92 • Gibraltar (UK)
93 • Greece

Where are we going to ?

94 • Greenland (Denmark)
95 • Grenada
96 • Guadeloupe (France)
97 • Guam (USA)
98 • Guatemala
99 • Guernsey (UK)
100 • Guinea-Bissau
101 • Guinea
102 • Guyana
103 • Haiti
104 • Honduras
105 • Hong-Kong (China)
106 • Hungary
107 • Iceland
108 • India
109 • Indonesia
110 • Iran
111 • Iraq
112 • Ireland
113 • Isle of Man (UK)
114 • Israel
115 • Italy
116 • Jamaica
117 • Japan
118 • Jersey (UK)
119 • Jordan
120 • Kazakhstan
121 • Kenya
122 • Kiribati
123 • Kosovo
124 • Kuwait
125 • Kyrgyzstan
126 • Laos
127 • Latvia
128 • Lebanon
129 • Lesotho
130 • Liberia
131 • Libya
132 • Liechtenstein
133 • Lithuania
134 • Luxembourg
135 • Macau (China)

136 • Madagascar
137 • Madeira (Portugal)
138 • Malawi
139 • Malaysia
140 • Maldives
141 • Mali
142 • Malta
143 • Marshall Islands (USA)
144 • Martinique (France)
145 • Mauritania
146 • Mauritius
147 • Mayotte (France)
148 • Mexico
149 • Micronesia
150 • Moldova
151 • Monaco
152 • Mongolia
153 • Montenegro
154 • Montserrat (UK)
155 • Morocco
156 • Mozambique
157 • Myanmar (Burma)
158 • Namibia
159 • Nauru
160 • Nepal
161 • Netherlands (the)
162 • New Caledonia (France)
163 • New Zealand
164 • Nicaragua
165 • Niger
166 • Nigeria
167 • Niue
168 • North Korea
169 • North Macedonia
170 • Northern Ireland (UK)
171 • Northern Mariana Islands (USA)
172 • Norway
173 • Oman
174 • Pakistan
175 • Palau
176 • Palestine
177 • Panama

Where are we going to ?

178 • Papua New Guinea
179 • Paraguay
180 • Peru
181 • Philippines
182 • Pitcairn Island (UK)
183 • Poland
184 • Portugal
185 • Puerto Rico (USA)
186 • Qatar
187 • Reunion Island (France)
188 • Romania
189 • Russia
190 • Rwanda
191 • Saba (Netherlands)
192 • Saint Kitts and Nevis
193 • Saint Lucia
194 • Saint Vincent and the Grenadines
195 • Samoa
196 • San Marino
197 • São Tome and Principe
198 • Saudi Arabia
199 • Scotland (UK)
200 • Senegal
201 • Serbia
202 • Seychelles
203 • Sierra Leone
204 • Singapore
205 • Slovakia
206 • Slovenia
207 • Solomon Islands
208 • Somalia
209 • South Africa
210 • South Korea
211 • South Sudan
212 • Spain
213 • Sri Lanka
214 • St Eustatius (Netherlands)
215 • St Marteen / St Martin (Netherlands / France)
216 • Sudan
217 • Suriname
218 • Sweden
219 • Switzerland
220 • Syria
221 • Taiwan
222 • Tajikistan
223 • Tanzania
224 • Thailand
225 • Tibet (China)
226 • Timor-Leste (East Timor)
227 • Togo
228 • Tokelau
229 • Tonga
230 • Trinidad and Tobago
231 • Tunisia
232 • Turkey
233 • Turkmenistan
234 • Turks and Caicos Islands (UK)
235 • Tuvalu
236 • Uganda
237 • Ukraine
238 • United Arab Emirates - Abu Dhabi
239 • United Arab Emirates - Dubai
240 • United States
241 • Uruguay
242 • US Virgin Islands (USA)
243 • Uzbekistan
244 • Vanuatu
245 • Vatican City
246 • Venezuela
247 • Vietnam
248 • Wales (UK)
249 • Wallis and Futuna (France)
250 • Western Sahara
251 • Yemen
252 • Zambia
253 • Zimbabwe

AFGHANISTAN

Central Asia
population: 42,919,968
Size (sq miles): 252,071
Size (sq km):   652,860

The Minaret of Jam: Standing at 65 meters tall in a remote area of Afghanistan, the Minaret of Jam is a mysterious and beautiful tower. Built in the 12th century, it's covered in intricate brickwork and inscriptions from the Quran. What's even more intriguing is that nobody knows for sure why it was built in such an isolated place. It's a true historical puzzle!

The National Game, Buzkashi: Imagine a game where horse-mounted players compete to grab a goat or calf carcass and drop it in a scoring circle. This is Buzkashi, Afghanistan's national sport. It's a thrilling and intense game, deeply rooted in Afghan culture. Players, called "Chapandaz," are highly respected and the game is a major event in Afghan society.

Afghan Cuisine: Afghani food is a delicious blend of influences from the Middle East and South Asia. One must-try dish is Kabuli Pulao, a fragrant rice dish cooked with raisins, carrots, and lamb. It's not just a meal; it's a celebration of flavors, often served during special occasions and gatherings, symbolizing hospitality and tradition.

ALBANIA

Eastern Europe
population: 2,828,548
Size (sq miles): 10,579
Size (sq km):   27,400

The City of a Thousand Windows: Berat, known as the "City of a Thousand Windows," is a stunning sight in Albania. This UNESCO World Heritage site is famous for its white Ottoman houses climbing up the hillside, all facing the Osum River. The windows of these houses seem to be stacked on top of each other, creating a picturesque and unique architectural style.

The Bunkers of Albania: Albania has over 170,000 bunkers! These small, dome-shaped concrete bunkers were built during the Cold War, when the country's leader feared invasion. They are scattered all across the countryside and beaches, serving as a unique reminder of Albania's past. Some have been transformed into cafes, museums, and even homes.

The Blue Eye Spring: Imagine a natural water spring so deep and clear that it looks like a bright blue eye. That's the Blue Eye Spring in southern Albania. It's a natural water spring with water so pure and blue, it seems almost magical. The exact depth is unknown, but it's believed to be over fifty meters deep. Surrounded by a forest, it's a perfect spot for nature lovers and a great example of Albania's stunning natural beauty.

ALGERIA

North Africa
population: 46,010,563
Size (sq miles): 919,595
Size (sq km):   2,381,740

The Sahara Desert: Algeria is home to a significant portion of the Sahara, the world's largest hot desert. This vast desert landscape is not just sand; it includes mountain ranges, rock formations, and even oases. The Sahara in Algeria is famous for its breathtaking beauty, especially during sunrise and sunset when the colors of the sands change dramatically.

The Ancient City of Timgad: Imagine a city founded by the Romans in 100 AD that's still standing today! Timgad, known as the "Pompeii of Africa," is a UNESCO World Heritage site. This ancient city was once a bustling metropolis and is remarkably well-preserved. Visitors can see the old streets, a theater, temples, and even an ancient library. It's like a live history book!

Couscous, a Culinary Staple: Couscous is not just a dish in Algeria; it's a cultural icon. This traditional food made from semolina wheat is often cooked with vegetables, spices, and sometimes meat or fish. It's central to family life and gatherings. In Algerian culture, couscous is more than food; it's a symbol of togetherness and tradition, often served during important celebrations.

AMERICAN SAMOA
United States

Oceania
population: 43,688
Size (sq miles): 77
Size (sq km):   200

The National Park of American Samoa: This is one of the most unique national parks in the U.S. system, covering parts of three islands. What makes it special is that it's home to both land and marine ecosystems. You can explore rainforests, beaches, and coral reefs, all in one park. The park protects many native species, including flying foxes, which are large, fruit-eating bats known for their impressive wingspan.

The 'Ava Ceremony: 'Ava (also known as kava) is a traditional ceremonial drink made from the ground root of the kava plant. In American Samoa, the 'ava ceremony is a crucial part of the culture, symbolizing respect and hospitality. It's often performed during important gatherings, welcoming guests, and marking significant events. The ceremony is a beautiful expression of Samoan tradition and community spirit.

Umu Cooking: The traditional way of cooking in American Samoa is called 'umu, which involves an earth oven. Food, often wrapped in banana leaves, is slow-cooked over hot stones buried in the ground. This method gives dishes like taro, breadfruit, and fish a unique, smoky flavor. Umu cooking is not just about food; it's a communal activity that brings families and communities together, showcasing the Samoan way of life.

ANDORRA

Western Europe
population: 80,241
Size (sq miles): 181
Size (sq km):   470

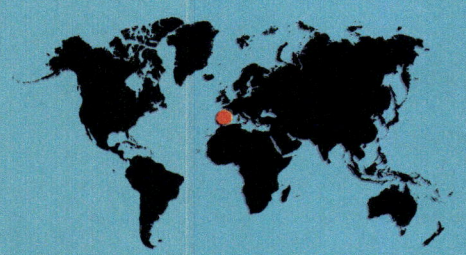

A **Country of Mountains:** Did you know that Andorra doesn't have a single airport due to its mountainous terrain? It's one of the world's smallest countries, but almost all of it is high in the mountains. The average elevation is an impressive 1,996 meters (6,549 feet) above sea level, making it a paradise for skiers and hikers.

The Church of Santa Coloma: Among Andorra's charming old churches, the Church of Santa Coloma stands out. It's one of the oldest, dating back to the 9th century, with a unique circular bell tower that's rare in the region. The church, with its simple yet beautiful stone architecture, is a window into the country's past.

The Dance of the Contrapàs: In Andorra, there's a traditional dance called the Contrapàs, which is especially popular in the town of Ordino. This dance is a centuries-old tradition, usually performed during the town's festival in September. Dancers wear colorful costumes and move to the rhythm of a cobla (traditional Catalan music band), showcasing Andorra's rich cultural heritage.

ANGOLA

Southern Africa
population: 37,355,498
Size (sq miles): 481,353
Size (sq km):   1,246,700

Mysterious Mountains and Desert Dunes: Angola is a land of contrasts! In the south, there's the Namib Desert, one of the world's oldest deserts, stretching along the Atlantic Ocean. Imagine endless golden sands meeting the deep blue sea! But that's not all. Angola is also home to the Tundavala Gap, a breathtaking cliff in the Huíla province. If you stand at the edge, you'll feel like you're at the top of the world, looking down on a vast, green valley and distant mountains.

The Giant Iron Lady of Angola: In the bustling capital city, Luanda, you'll find an impressive statue known as 'The Iron Woman'. It's not just any statue; it's a symbol of resistance and strength. This monument is a tribute to a powerful 17th-century Angolan queen, Njinga Mbande, who bravely fought against colonial forces. The statue captures her determination and is a source of inspiration for many Angolans.

A Colorful Celebration of Culture: One of the most vibrant customs in Angola is the Carnival of Luanda. It's a festival full of life, just like Brazil's famous carnival! Every year, streets come alive with colorful costumes, energetic dances, and rhythmic music. It's a time when people from all over the country, young and old, come together to celebrate Angolan culture and history through dance, song, and parades. This carnival isn't just a party; it's a display of the rich traditions and diverse cultures that make Angola unique.

ANGUILLA
United Kingdom

Central America - Carribbean
population: 15,921
Size (sq miles): 35
Size (sq km): 90

Beaches Galore: Anguilla is a beach lover's paradise, with over 33 stunning beaches! Rendezvous Bay is a standout, stretching over 2.5 miles with soft, white sand and crystal-clear waters. It's perfect for swimming, sunbathing, or just marveling at the gorgeous Caribbean Sea. Each beach on this small island has its own charm, making Anguilla a dream destination for those who love the sun, sand, and sea.

The Historic Wallblake House: In the heart of Anguilla stands Wallblake House, a piece of living history. Built in 1787, it's the oldest and only surviving plantation house on the island. This well-preserved structure gives a unique glimpse into Anguilla's past. It's not just a building; it's a storybook of the island's colonial era, offering insights into the daily lives of its early inhabitants.

The Boat Racing Tradition: Anguilla is crazy about boat racing! It's the national sport and a deep-rooted cultural tradition. Imagine sleek, colorful boats slicing through the blue waters, powered by teamwork and the spirit of competition. During major festivals like Anguilla Day, the excitement is contagious, with everyone from kids to grandparents cheering for their favorite boats. This thrilling sport is more than a race; it's a celebration of the island's maritime heritage and community spirit.

ANTARCTICA

Antarctica
population: 0
Size (sq miles): 5,500,000
Size (sq km):   14,200,000

No Polar Bears, Just Science!: First things first, if you're packing a camera to snap pictures of polar bears, you're heading to the wrong pole! Antarctica is the only continent (with Africa) without polar bears. Instead, it's the ultimate chill zone for scientists from around the world. They're busy studying everything from climate change to penguins, who, by the way, are the real locals here!

The Moving Post Office: Think your local post office is busy? Wait till you hear about Port Lockroy, Antarctica's own postal center! It's housed in a tiny museum and processes over 70,000 postcards each year sent by visitors to over 100 countries. So, if you want to send a chilly greeting from the coldest place on Earth, you know where to go!

Midnight Sun and Polar Night: Forget about setting your alarm clock – in Antarctica, the sun doesn't play by the rules. During the summer, the sun shines 24/7, creating the famous 'Midnight Sun'. But in winter, it's time for the 'Polar Night', where the sun takes a long break and it's night-time round the clock. Talk about confusing your body clock!

ANTIGUA AND BARBUDA

Central America - Carribbean
population: 94,612
Size (sq miles): 170
Size (sq km):   440

Beach for Every Day of the Year: If you're planning to visit a new beach every day in Antigua, you better have a year off! This sunny island boasts 365 beaches - one for each day of the year. They say variety is the spice of life, and with so many beaches, you're in for a spicy Caribbean adventure. Just don't forget which beach you started with!

A Tasty Monument – The Pineapple!: While many countries have statues or buildings as national symbols, Antigua claims the delicious pineapple! The Antigua Black Pineapple, known for being super sweet (just like the locals), is a symbol of the island's unique flavors. Who needs a stone monument when you can have a fruit that's both a treat and a symbol?

Cricket Isn't Just a Game, It's a Party!: In Antigua and Barbuda, cricket is not just a sport; it's a festival, a community event, and a reason to party. When there's a match, everyone from toddlers to grandparents becomes a cricket expert. The stadiums turn into a sea of color, music, and dance - it's like a carnival that celebrates every run and wicket!

ARGENTINA

South America
population: 45,946,075
Size (sq miles): 1,056,641
Size (sq km):   2,736,690

The Dancing Streets of Buenos Aires: In Argentina, even the sidewalks seem to sway to the rhythm of Tango. This passionate dance started in Buenos Aires and has since twirled its way into the hearts of people worldwide. Imagine couples dancing on the city streets, as if they've got their own portable dancefloors under their feet!

A Sweet Tooth's Heaven – Dulce de Leche: Argentinians have a secret weapon in the world of sweets - Dulce de Leche. This creamy caramel spread is like a national treasure. It's in desserts, on toast, and sometimes just straight off the spoon (we won't tell!). They say too much of anything is bad, but in Argentina, they haven't heard that about Dulce de Leche!

Football: More Than a Game, It's a Lifestyle: In Argentina, football (soccer) isn't just a sport; it's a lifestyle, a religion, and probably a way to determine one's future friendships. The passion for football runs deep, with fans cheering for their teams with a fervor that could power a small city. It's not just about winning; it's about living and breathing every moment of the game!

ARMENIA

West Asia
population: 2,777,975
Size (sq miles): 10,992
Size (sq km): 28,470

A Country of Firsts - Really Old Wine!: Armenia takes "aged wine" to a whole new level. It's home to the world's oldest winery, found in the Areni cave, dating back over 6,000 years. That's right, Armenians were making wine while the rest of the world was still figuring out farming. Talk about being ahead of the times in the wine department!

Chess Wizards in the Making: In Armenia, chess is not just a game; it's a school subject! Yes, you heard it right. Armenian kids learn to say "checkmate" before they can even do long division. By the time they're teenagers, they're probably plotting world domination on the chessboard.

The Cascading Wonder of Yerevan: The Cascade in Yerevan is a giant stairway that seems to climb right into the clouds. It's not just a staircase; it's a fitness challenge, an art gallery, and a social hub all rolled into one. If you climb to the top, you're rewarded with stunning views of the city and Mount Ararat (weather permitting). Just remember, what goes up must come down - unless you find the hidden escalators!

ARUBA
The Netherlands

Central America - Carribbean
population: 106,216
Size (sq miles): 69
Size (sq km):   180

A Bridge Not Built by Hands: In Aruba, there's a bridge unlike any other – the Natural Bridge. Now, while it may have collapsed in 2005, it still stands as a testament to nature's architecture skills. Formed by years of wind and waves, this limestone creation was once the island's natural wonder. Today, its remains still draw visitors, proving that even in collapse, it's a star!

Divi-Divi Trees: The Natural Compass: Need directions in Aruba? Just look at the Divi-Divi trees! These quirky trees consistently point southwest due to the trade winds that blow across the island. It's like nature's own compass, except it doesn't fit in your pocket and it's pretty bad at giving street names.

Carnival: A Festival of Color and Calypso: In Aruba, Carnival isn't just a party; it's a season! It's like the island turns into one big dance floor, with people dressed in feathers and glitter, moving to the beat of calypso and soca music. For weeks, life is a parade of music, dance, and elaborate costumes, proving that Arubans take their fun as seriously as their relaxation!

AUSTRALIA

Oceania
population: 26,596,701
Size (sq miles): 2,966,151
Size (sq km):   7,682,300

The Great, Big, Really Big Reef: First off, Australia is home to the Great Barrier Reef, the largest living thing on Earth. It's so big, astronauts can see it from space! It's like the universe's own snorkeling spot, complete with colorful coral, fish, and the occasional curious sea turtle asking for directions.

Big Things – Literally: Australia loves its 'Big Things' – gigantic replicas of everyday objects. There's the Big Banana, the Big Pineapple, and even the Big Merino sheep! It's like Australia's way of saying, "Go big or go home," to the rest of the world's monuments.

A Sporty Nation Indeed: Australians are sports-crazy – whether it's cricket, rugby, or Aussie Rules football. They say if you're not playing a sport, you're probably at the beach, watching a sport, or at least thinking about sport. And if you ever get into a debate about which sport is best, just remember: in Australia, every sport is the best... as long as it's winning!

AUSTRIA

Western Europe
population: 8,970,006
Size (sq miles): 31,818
Size (sq km):   82,409

The Hills Are Alive, But The Mountains Are Breathtaking: Austria is famous for its stunning Alps, where you can ski, hike, or just yodel your heart out (okay, maybe not the yodeling). These mountains aren't just for show – they're a playground for adventurers and nature lovers. And let's not forget, they were the real stars of "The Sound of Music"!

A Cake Worth Starting a War Over: The Sachertorte, a delectable chocolate cake with apricot jam, is so famous it once caused a legal battle! This cake isn't just a dessert; it's a piece of Austrian pride. Cafés in Vienna have been serving it for centuries, and no visit is complete without a slice... or two.

Dancing Horses and Classical Music: Vienna, the capital, is not just about grand palaces and historic streets. It's also home to the Spanish Riding School, where you can watch horses perform ballet! Yes, you read that right – horses doing ballet. And as for music, Austria was the playground for composers like Mozart and Beethoven, making it a classical music fan's dream come true. In Austria, it's perfectly normal to hum a symphony while watching a horse pirouette!

AZERBAIJAN

West Asia
population: 10,443,143
Size (sq miles): 31,914
Size (sq km):   82,658

A Flaming Mountain - Literally!: In Azerbaijan, you can find a mountain that's on fire. Yes, Yanar Dag is a natural gas fire which blazes continuously on a hillside. It's like Azerbaijan decided to have a barbecue and accidentally set a mountain on fire. But don't worry, it's been burning for thousands of years, so they're pretty used to it by now!

Mugham Music - Not Your Average Pop Song: Azerbaijan is famous for Mugham, a traditional genre of music. It's a complex form of art, combining poetry and improvisational singing. It's like jazz, if jazz decided to get really introspective and philosophical. Attending a Mugham performance is like taking a musical journey through Azerbaijan's soul.

A Sport That's More Slippery Than Wrestling: Ever heard of oil wrestling? In Azerbaijan, it's a traditional sport called Gulesh. Wrestlers cover themselves in oil, making it a slippery challenge to get a good grip. It's like trying to catch a fish with your bare hands, but the fish is a muscular guy in a leather trouser. It's a test of strength, skill, and probably who's the best at doing laundry afterwards.

AZORES
Portugal

Europe · Atlantic
population: 236,440
Size (sq miles): 908
Size (sq km):   2,351

More Cows Than People? Mooo-ve Over!: In the Azores, cows might be running the show. There are more cows than people on these lush islands, making it a paradise for dairy lovers. Imagine cows leisurely grazing on green hills with ocean views – talk about living the dream! You haven't experienced the Azores until you've tasted their cheese, which the cows probably brag about.

Europe's Only Tea Plantation – A Brew-tiful Sight: Love tea? The Azores is home to Europe's only tea plantations. Gorreana Tea Plantation has been growing tea since the 19th century. Here, you can stroll among tea bushes, learn how tea is made, and sip on a fresh brew. It's like being in a giant green tea cup, but with better scenery.

Underwater Volcanoes - Dive Into the Deep: The Azores is a hotspot for diving – literally. The islands are dotted with underwater volcanic vents, creating an otherworldly seascape. It's like snorkeling in a science fiction movie, except the colorful fish and thermal vents are real. So, put on your flippers and dive into an adventure where the mountain peaks are below the waves!

BAHAMAS

Carribbean
population: 412,628
Size (sq miles): 5,383
Size (sq km):   13,943

Pig Beach - The Real 'Hog' Heaven: In the Bahamas, pigs don't just roll in the mud, they swim in the sea! At Big Major Cay, you can find the famous swimming pigs. These porky paddlers are not shy about making a splash and are always ready for their close-up. It's the only place where you can go to the beach and leave with a selfie that makes your friends go, "Wait, is that a pig in the ocean?"

The Staircase to... Well, More Staircase: In Nassau, there's a famous staircase called the Queen's Staircase. Carved out of solid limestone by slaves in the late 18th century, it has 65 steps – one for each year of Queen Victoria's reign. Climbing it is like stepping back in time, except with a lot more panting and less royal attire.

Junkanoo: A Festival of Feathers, Glitter, and Good Vibes: If you thought New Year's Eve was just fireworks, think again! In the Bahamas, they celebrate Junkanoo, an explosion of color, music, and dance. Picture people dressed in elaborate costumes, dancing in the streets to the beat of drums and cowbells. It's like Mardi Gras and a costume party had a baby that really loves to dance.

BAHRAIN

Middle East
population: 1,463,265
Size (sq miles): 303.7
Size (sq km):   786.5

The Land of Ancient Pearls: Bahrain is known as the land of pearls, and it's not because they have a great jewelry store. For thousands of years, people have been diving into the Persian Gulf here to find natural pearls. Imagine telling your friends, "I got these pearls from the sea," instead of, "I got these at the mall." It's like ancient treasure hunting, but with more oysters and less pirates.

The Tree of Life - Nature's Own Mystery: In the middle of Bahrain's desert, there stands a 400-year-old tree, the Tree of Life. It's famous because it survives without an apparent water source. It's like the tree version of a survival expert, living off the grid and loving it. Visitors often wonder if it knows the secret to eternal life, or at least how to survive a week without watering the plants.

Formula One - A 1001 nights fiesta: Bahrain's Formula One Grand Prix isn't just about fast cars; it's a party on wheels. Held at night under bright lights (because days are too hot), it feels more like a high-speed carnival. It's a mix of high-octane racing, concerts, and an atmosphere buzzing with excitement, or maybe that's just the sound of the engines. For Bahrain, it's party central.

BANGLADESH

South Asia
population: 169,828,911
Size (sq miles): 57,320
Size (sq km): 148,460

A Country Carved by Rivers: Bangladesh is like a grand waterpark, but natural! It's a land crisscrossed by about 700 rivers, making it the perfect place for a game of 'spot the land'. These rivers are like busy highways, but instead of cars, there are boats of all shapes and sizes. Whether it's the mighty Padma or the historic Meghna, each river has its own story to tell.

The Artistic Rickshaws: In Bangladesh, rickshaws aren't just a mode of transport; they're moving art galleries! These colorful rickshaws are hand-painted with vibrant scenes, from rural life to pop culture. Riding one is like being in a parade float, except it's a regular Tuesday, and you're just trying to get to the market.

Home to the Royal Bengal Tiger: The Sundarbans, the largest mangrove forest in the world, is the royal residence of the majestic Bengal tiger. But don't expect a palace; these tigers are wild and free, ruling over a kingdom of dense forests and winding rivers. Spotting one is like seeing nature's own celebrity – just remember, no autographs, please!

BARBADOS

Carribbean
population: 281,998
Size (sq miles): 169
Size (sq km):   439

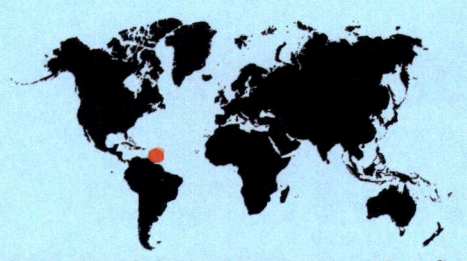

Flying Fish - Not Just in Cartoons: In Barbados, fish don't just swim; they fly! The island is famous for its flying fish, which leap out of the water and glide through the air. It's like they're trying to evolve into birds, but haven't quite figured out the landing part yet. A trip to Barbados isn't complete without trying the national dish: flying fish with cou-cou, which thankfully, stays on the plate.

Windmills with a Twist: Barbados is dotted with old sugar windmills, a reminder of its sugar plantation past. One of the most famous is Morgan Lewis Windmill, one of the only two working sugar windmills in the world. It's like stepping into a postcard, except the windmill is real, and you don't have to squeeze into the picture.

Cricket More Than a Sport, It's a Lifestyle: Barbadians, or Bajans, are mad about cricket. It's not just a sport; it's a national passion. On any given day, you'll find locals passionately discussing the latest match. It's like a religion, except the gods wield cricket bats and wear pads. And if you get the chance to watch a match, remember, cheering for a six is mandatory!

BELARUS

Eastern Europe
population: 9,255,524
Size (sq miles): 80,153
Size (sq km):   207,595

The Land of Lush Bogs: Think of Belarus and you might not immediately think of... bogs. But this country is a bog superstar, with vast, lush peatlands that are like nature's sponges. It's where plants and animals chill out in the squishy, wet wonderland. Going bog-walking in Belarus is like stepping into a squelchy, green version of a waterbed - except with more frogs and less sleep.

The Mighty Mir Castle: Belarus isn't short on fairy tale scenes, and the Mir Castle Complex is straight out of a storybook. This UNESCO World Heritage site looks like it was designed by a medieval architect who really loved towers and turrets. Visiting the castle is like stepping back in time, except you don't have to worry about pesky dragons or knights challenging you to a duel.

Potato Lovers Unite!: If there were a potato fan club, Belarus would be the president. Belarusians love their potatoes, and they've got over 300 different potato dishes to prove it. From draniki (potato pancakes) to babka (potato pie), it's like every meal is a potato party. In Belarus, 'meat and potatoes' isn't just a meal; it's a way of life!

BELGIUM

Western Europe
population: 11,697,557
Size (sq miles): 11,849
Size (sq km):   30,689

Waffle Wonderland: In Belgium, waffles aren't just a breakfast treat; they're a national treasure. Here, you'll find street vendors serving up hot, crispy waffles topped with everything from strawberries to chocolate. It's like every day is a waffle party, and everyone's invited. But remember, Belgian waffles are so good, you might forget about the other Belgian delights!

The Adventures of Tintin and Friends: Belgium is the birthplace of some of the world's most famous comic book characters, like Tintin, Smurfs, and Lucky Luke. It's like the entire country was bitten by a radioactive illustrator – suddenly, everyone's drawing comics! In Brussels, you can even follow a comic strip route and see your favorite characters painted on buildings. It's a bit like walking inside a giant comic book.

Manneken Pis – The Cheeky Icon: No visit to Belgium is complete without seeing Manneken Pis, the famous statue of a little boy... well, peeing. He's a tiny guy with a big reputation and is often dressed in costumes. This little fellow is so loved, he has over 900 outfits! Talk about a fashion icon with a quirky sense of humor.

BELIZE

Central America
population: 441,471
Size (sq miles): 8,867
Size (sq km):   22,966

The Land of the Jaguar: Belize is a paradise for jaguars, the largest cat in the Americas. The Cockscomb Basin Wildlife Sanctuary is known as the world's first jaguar preserve. It's like a VIP club for big cats, where jaguars roam free, and the monkeys are always on the lookout. If you're lucky, you might spot one lounging around, probably wondering why humans don't have spots.

Ancient Mayan Cities in the Jungle: Belize is home to impressive Mayan ruins like Caracol and Xunantunich. These ancient cities are hidden in the lush jungle, giving them a 'lost world' vibe. Visiting them is like stepping back in time, if time travel involved more mosquitoes and less science fiction.

Rice and Beans, The Belizean Way: In Belize, rice and beans are a staple, but it's not just any rice and beans. Cooked in coconut milk and served with spicy stewed chicken, this dish is a flavor fiesta. It's like the Belizean version of comfort food, and it's understood that a meal isn't complete without it. Just remember, it's "rice and beans," not "beans and rice" – the order matters!

BENIN

West Africa
population: 13,754,688
Size (sq miles): 44,310
Size (sq km):   114,763

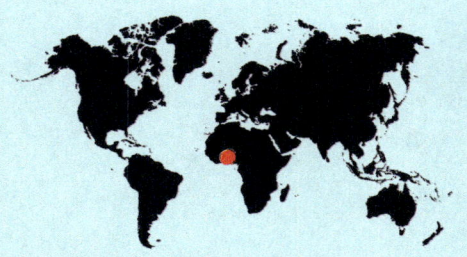

The Ancient Kingdom of Dahomey: In Benin, history buffs can get their fill at the Royal Palaces of Abomey. These palaces were once the heart of the powerful Dahomey Kingdom. Visiting them is like stepping into a time machine, except with fewer buttons and more ancient artifacts. The walls tell stories of past kings and their epic deeds – think Game of Thrones, but in West Africa and without the dragons.

Voodoo: More Than Just Magic: Benin is the birthplace of Voodoo, and here, it's a recognized religion, not just the stuff of spooky tales. Voodoo ceremonies are a mix of music, dance, and rituals – it's like a spiritual party, and everyone's invited. Don't be surprised if you see a Voodoo priest in full regalia; it's all part of the local charm.

The Colorful Dantokpa Market: Want to shop like a local? Head to Cotonou's Dantokpa Market, one of West Africa's largest markets. It's a kaleidoscope of colors and a symphony of sounds. From exotic spices to handmade fabrics, it's like a treasure trove for the senses. Remember, bargaining is part of the fun, so put on your haggling hat and dive into the hustle and bustle!

BERMUDA
United Kingdom

North America
population: 63,913
Size (sq miles): 20.5
Size (sq km): 53.2

Not Just Any Sand – It's Pink!: Bermuda isn't your average beach destination. Here, the sands blush with a pinkish hue, thanks to tiny red organisms that live on the coral reefs. It's like Mother Nature decided to try out a new color palette. These pink beaches aren't just for sunbathing; they're perfect for that Instagram-worthy shot where you say, "No filter needed!"

The Bermuda Triangle: More Mystery Than Menace: Bermuda lends its name to the infamous Bermuda Triangle, a region known for mysterious shipwrecks and airplane disappearances. While the tales are spooky, don't worry – it's more of a myth than a reality. Visiting Bermuda is like stepping into an adventure novel, but with less drama and more relaxation.

Bermuda Shorts: Official Business Attire: In Bermuda, shorts aren't just casual wear; they're a fashion statement. Paired with a blazer and knee-high socks, Bermuda shorts are official business attire here. It's like someone decided that meetings would be more fun if everyone looked like they were heading to a garden party afterward. And really, who could argue with that?

BHUTAN

South Asia
population: 777,486
Size (sq miles): 14,824
Size (sq km): 38,394

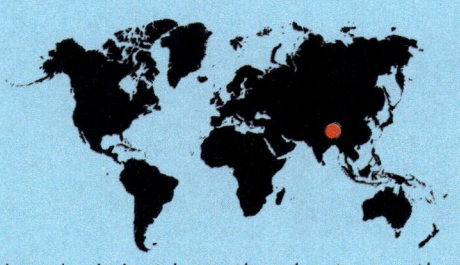

The Dragon in the Clouds: In Bhutan, they don't just have thunderstorms; they have the "Thunder Dragon". That's right, Bhutan is also known as 'Druk Yul' – Land of the Thunder Dragon – because of the fierce storms that roll in from the Himalayas. It's like the weather has its own mythical creature, making every thunderclap a bit more dramatic.

Dzongs: Not Just Fortresses, But Architectural Wonders: Bhutan's dzongs are a sight to behold. These massive fortresses, part monastery, part government office, are masterpieces of Bhutanese architecture. Visiting a dzong is like stepping into a time where monks, warriors, and bureaucrats mingled in corridors adorned with beautiful paintings. It's the ultimate multi-purpose building, ancient style.

Gross National Happiness – More Important Than Money: Bhutan measures success not just by Gross Domestic Product, but by Gross National Happiness. That's right, happiness is a serious business here! It's like the government is a happiness coach, ensuring policies contribute to the well-being of its people. In Bhutan, "How happy are you?" might just be as common a question as "How are you?"

BOLIVIA

South America
population: 12,186,079
Size (sq miles): 424,164
Size (sq km):   1,098,581

The Land of Extreme Landscapes: Bolivia is the country where geography went wild. It's home to Salar de Uyuni, the world's largest salt flat, which turns into a giant mirror when it rains. Then there's Lake Titicaca, the highest navigable lake on Earth, where you might need to catch your breath – not just from the views, but also the altitude. It's like nature decided to show off all its tricks in one place!

A Potato for Every Occasion: Love potatoes? Welcome to paradise! Bolivia has over 2000 varieties of potatoes – that's right, two thousand! It's like every potato had a family reunion and decided to settle down here. From colorful ones to ones that taste like apples, there's a potato for every mood.

Zebra Crossings, Literally: In the bustling streets of La Paz, you might be helped across the road by... a zebra! Well, not an actual zebra, but a person dressed as one. These 'zebra' traffic assistants are part of a quirky initiative to help with road safety. They dance, they mime, and they make crossing the street an unexpected safari adventure.

BONAIRE
The Netherlands

Carribbean
population: 24,098
Size (sq miles): 111
Size (sq km): 288

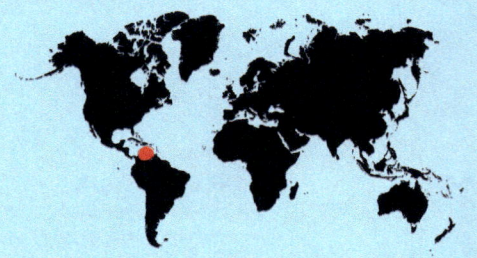

Flamingo Airport - Where Birds Have Right of Way: On Bonaire, flamingos are not just another pretty bird; they're almost like local celebrities. The island even named its airport after them – Flamingo International Airport. Here, these pink-feathered friends have the right of way, and spotting them is like seeing nature's own VIPs strutting down a pink carpet.

Mountains of Salt: Nature's Seasoning Shaker: Bonaire is famous for its striking salt pans, where you'll find mountains of pure, white salt. They look like someone spilled a giant salt shaker on the island. These salt pyramids aren't just for show; they're a big part of the island's economy. And let's be honest, they make for a pretty surreal landscape.

Snorkel to Send a Postcard: Ever wanted to mail a postcard underwater? On Bonaire, you can! The island boasts the world's only underwater post office. So, grab your snorkel, dive down, and send a greeting from the deep blue. It's like Aquaman's version of a mailbox, but with more fish and fewer superheroes.

BOSNIA AND HERZEGOVINA

Eastern Europe
population: 3,475,000
Size (sq miles): 19,780
Size (sq km): 51,229

The Old Bridge of Mostar - A Leap into History: In the heart of Bosnia and Herzegovina lies the Old Bridge of Mostar, a stunningly picturesque bridge that looks like it's straight out of a fairy tale. But it's not just for crossing – it's also for jumping! Every year, brave souls participate in a diving competition, leaping 24 meters into the river below. It's like the local version of bungee jumping, minus the bungee.

Coffee Time is Serious Business: In Bosnia and Herzegovina, drinking coffee is an art form and a social ritual. It's not just about the caffeine kick; it's about sitting down, chatting, and savoring every sip. The coffee comes in a džezva (a small metal pot) with a side of time travel – as each sip takes you back to centuries-old traditions.

Sarajevo's Abandoned Bobsleigh Track - An Olympic Ghost Story: Once upon the 1984 Winter Olympics, Sarajevo built a state-of-the-art bobsleigh track. Today, it's an eerie yet fascinating relic of the past, covered in graffiti and surrounded by nature. It's like a concrete snake winding through the forest – a playground for hikers and urban explorers. Just remember, it's BYOB (Bring Your Own Bobsleigh).

BOTSWANA

Southern Africa
population: 2,675,352
Size (sq miles): 224,610
Size (sq km): 581,730

Elephant Traffic Jams Are a Thing: In Botswana, you might get stuck in a 'traffic jam' – but not the kind you're used to. Here, it's the elephants that rule the roads. Chobe National Park is home to one of the largest elephant populations in the world. Watching these gentle giants roam freely is like witnessing a majestic parade, but remember, no honking at the elephants!

The Okavango Delta: A Wet Desert Miracle: Imagine a river that flows into a desert but never reaches the sea. That's the Okavango Delta for you – a lush, watery oasis in the midst of the Kalahari Desert. It's a haven for wildlife and a geography teacher's dream case study. The delta is like nature's own water park, except the slides are replaced with hippos and crocodiles.

Dancing Is Serious Business: In Botswana, traditional dance is more than just moving to music; it's a way of life. The 'polka' and 'setapa' dances are energetic, vibrant, and involve a lot of foot-stomping. It's like a fitness class, but with more rhythm and cultural heritage. If you're ever invited to join in, just remember: it's less about the steps and more about the spirit!

BRAZIL

South America
population: 203,062,512
Size (sq miles): 3,287,956
Size (sq km): 8,515,767

The Amazon Rainforest - Nature's Own Theme Park: In Brazil, you'll find the Amazon Rainforest, the world's largest tropical rainforest. It's like Mother Nature's version of a theme park, complete with a dizzying array of wildlife, towering trees, and rivers that double as roads. Forget roller coasters; here, a boat ride through the jungle or a monkey sighting is your adrenaline rush!

Christ the Redeemer: A Big Hug from Rio: Overlooking Rio de Janeiro is the iconic Christ the Redeemer statue, standing tall with arms wide open as if giving the whole city a hug. It's not just a marvel of engineering; it's like a selfie checkpoint for the whole world. And let's be honest, it probably has the best view in town.

Samba: Not Just a Dance, but a Way of Life: In Brazil, samba is more than a dance; it's the rhythm of life. During Carnival, the streets become a sea of color, music, and dance, with everyone moving to the beat of samba. It's like the country turns into one big dance floor. Whether you're a pro or have two left feet, in Brazil, samba is for everyone – it's all about the joy of movement!

BRITISH VIRGIN ISLANDS
United Kingdom

Carribbean
population: 30,030
Size (sq miles): 59
Size (sq km): 153

Pirate Lore and Sunken Ships: The British Virgin Islands (BVI) were once a favorite hangout for pirates like Blackbeard and Captain Kidd. Today, you might not find pirates, but you can explore shipwrecks and hidden coves – it's like a treasure hunt minus the treasure map. And who knows, maybe you'll stumble upon a forgotten pirate's chest, but more likely a great snorkeling spot!

The Baths: Nature's Own Maze: On Virgin Gorda, you'll find The Baths, a seaside area where giant boulders create natural tidal pools, tunnels, and arches. It's like nature's own version of a funhouse, but with better views and less clowns. Exploring The Baths is like playing hide and seek, except the ocean's in on the game.

Island Hopping: With over 60 islands and cays, the BVI is perfect for island hopping. You can't go wrong as all islands are what you expect of a postcard perfect holiday landscape. Whether by sailboat, ferry, or kayak, each island offers its own unique slice of paradise – just remember where you parked your boat!

BRUNEI

Southeast Asia
population: 460,345
Size (sq miles): 2,226
Size (sq km):   5,765

The Empire of the Rainforest: In Brunei, the rainforest is not just a backdrop; it's the main event. Over 70% of the country is covered in lush, untouched rainforest. It's like Mother Nature's own kingdom, complete with a chorus of birds, monkeys, and maybe the odd 'rainforest traffic jam' caused by wandering wildlife. Exploring Brunei's rainforests is like stepping into a green wonderland, minus the Mad Hatter.

The Shimmering Omar Ali Saifuddien Mosque: Brunei's capital, Bandar Seri Begawan, is home to one of the most stunning mosques in Southeast Asia. With its golden domes and crystal chandeliers, the Omar Ali Saifuddien Mosque looks like it's been plucked from a fairy tale. It's so shiny, you might need sunglasses just to admire it!

Ambuyat: Brunei's National Dish, a Sticky Affair: Ambuyat is a unique Bruneian delicacy made from the interior trunk of the sago palm. This sticky, glue-like dish is eaten with a bamboo fork called a 'candas'. It's an acquired taste, kind of like Brunei's answer to chewing gum, but for dinner. Eating Ambuyat is a fun challenge - it's like trying to eat a meal that's constantly trying to escape your fork.

BULGARIA

Eastern Europe
population: 6,447,710
Size (sq miles): 42,854.9
Size (sq km): 110,993.6

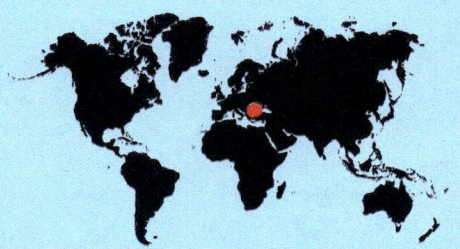

The Valley of Roses – Where Flowers Turn into Fragrance: In Bulgaria, there's a whole valley where roses rule. The Rose Valley is famous for producing some of the best rose oil in the world. It's like the flowers got together and decided to start a perfume business. Every year, there's even a Rose Festival – imagine a beauty pageant, but for roses and without the swimsuit competition.

Rila Monastery: A Hidden Gem Among the Mountains: Tucked away in the Rila Mountains lies the Rila Monastery, a stunning example of Bulgarian Renaissance architecture. With its colorful frescoes and towering peaks, it's like stepping into a hidden kingdom. It's so picturesque, it could be on a postcard – if postcards came with a soundtrack of monks chanting.

Yogurt: Bulgaria's Superfood: Bulgarians love their yogurt, and they've been making it for centuries. It's not just a breakfast food; it's a national treasure, loaded with healthy bacteria. Bulgarians might just attribute their longevity to this creamy delight. It's like their version of an elixir of life, but tastier and goes well with fruit.

BURKINA FASO

West Africa
population: 22,489,126
Size (sq miles): 105,878
Size (sq km): 274,223

The Warm Heart of West Africa: Burkina Faso, known as the "Land of Upright People," is not just upright but outright friendly. The country is famed for its warm hospitality, where smiles are as common as the hot sun. It's like the entire nation attended a charm school, and everyone graduated with honors. Visiting Burkina Faso is like being in a never-ending episode of 'Everybody Loves Everybody.'

Festima – A Festival of Masks and Mystique: In Burkina Faso, masks aren't just for Halloween. The Festival of Masks (Festima) is a spectacular cultural event where dancers don colorful masks, each telling a story of ancestral myths and social morals. It's like comic-con, but with more folklore and fewer superheroes.

Ouagadougou – The Cinematic Heart of Africa: Ouagadougou, the capital, hosts one of Africa's most important film festivals, FESPACO. Here, filmmakers from across the continent showcase their work, turning the city into a hub of African cinema. It's like the Oscars, but with more emphasis on storytelling and cultural heritage, and less on who wore it best.

BURUNDI

East Africa
population: 13,162,952
Size (sq miles): 10,747
Size (sq km): 27,834

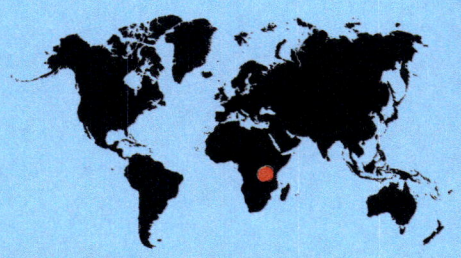

The Heartbeat of Burundi - The Royal Drummers: In Burundi, drums are not just musical instruments; they're a national symbol. The Royal Drummers of Burundi are world-famous, turning drumming into an athletic and artistic spectacle. It's like a full-body workout with a rhythm – imagine a gym class where everyone's in sync and on beat!

A Country of a Thousand Hills: Burundi might not have the tallest mountains, but it sure has plenty of hills. It's known as the 'Land of a Thousand Hills', so expect your legs to get a good workout just by walking around. The rolling landscapes are not just a feast for the eyes but also a challenge for anyone who mistakenly thinks it's all flat terrain.

Running: A National Pastime and Pride: Burundians don't just run; they excel at it. The country has produced some of the world's top long-distance runners. It's like the national sport is 'catch me if you can'. In Burundi, if you're not running, you're probably cheering for someone who is. It's a place where the phrase "going for a quick run" takes on a whole new meaning.

CABO VERDE

Africa
population: 561,901
Size (sq miles): 1,557
Size (sq km): 4,033

Island Hopping with a Musical Twist: In Cabo Verde, each island has its own unique rhythm. From the morna of Cesária Évora's São Vicente to the upbeat funaná of Santiago, music is the soul of these islands. It's like each island is a different track on a hit album, with Mother Nature as the producer. Island hopping here doesn't just mean a change of scenery, but a whole new soundtrack!

Pico do Fogo – A Friendly Neighborhood Volcano: Pico do Fogo, an active volcano, is the highest peak in Cabo Verde. Its last eruption was in 2014, but it's generally a well-behaved volcano. Climbing it is an adventure - like a hike with an added thrill of telling your friends you scaled an active volcano. And don't worry, it's not the "explodey" kind of active.

Grogue – The Spirit of Cabo Verde: Grogue, a local sugarcane spirit, is more than just a drink in Cabo Verde; it's a tradition. Distilled in rustic, roadside trapiches, this potent brew is the island's version of a warm welcome. It's said that grogue can fuel dance moves you never knew you had. Just remember, grogue might make you feel like a dancer, but it won't necessarily make you a good one!

CAMBODIA

Southeast Asia
population: 16,713,015
Size (sq miles): 69,898
Size (sq km): 181,035

Angkor Wat - A Temple That's on Everyone's Bucket List: In Cambodia, there's a temple so grand it's on the national flag. Angkor Wat is not just big; it's the largest religious monument in the world. Exploring its ruins is like stepping into a real-life Indiana Jones movie, minus the rolling boulders and with more selfie sticks.

Tuk-Tuk Rides: Cambodia's Twisty, Turny Taxis: In Cambodia, the tuk-tuk is king of the road. These little three-wheeled wonders zip through the streets, offering a ride that's part taxi, part roller coaster, and part 'hold-on-to-your-hats!' It's the best way to see the city - just as long as you don't mind playing a game of 'dodge the pothole.'

Karaoke: A National Pastime: Cambodians love karaoke, and it's not just confined to bars and living rooms. You'll find karaoke on buses, in parks, and even in some restaurants. It's like the whole country is auditioning for a national singing contest, where enthusiasm counts more than pitch. So, grab a mic and join in – in Cambodia, everyone's a superstar in waiting!

CAMEROON

Central Africa
population: 30,135,732
Size (sq miles): 183,569
Size (sq km): 475,442

The Country That Plays All of Africa's Geographies: Cameroon is like a mini version of the entire African continent. It's got a bit of everything – beaches, deserts, mountains, rainforests, and savannas. It's as if Mother Nature used Cameroon as a canvas to showcase her best work. So, whether you're a beach bum or a mountain hiker, Cameroon has got you covered. Just pack for all weather types!

Football: A National Obsession: In Cameroon, football (soccer) is not just a sport; it's a religion. The national team, the Indomitable Lions, are national heroes. On match days, the country virtually stops, and streets are deserted – everyone's glued to the screen. It's like a national holiday, and every goal is pure madness.

Cameroonian Fashion: Bright, Bold, and Beautiful: Cameroonian traditional attire is a festival of colors. From the grand boubou to the elegant pagnes, these outfits are not just clothes; they're artworks you can wear. Donning these vibrant fabrics is like saying, "Here I am, world!" But be warned, after wearing them, your regular clothes might seem a bit... well, boring.

CANADA

North America
population: 40,528,396
Size (sq miles): 3,855,100
Size (sq km):   9,984,670

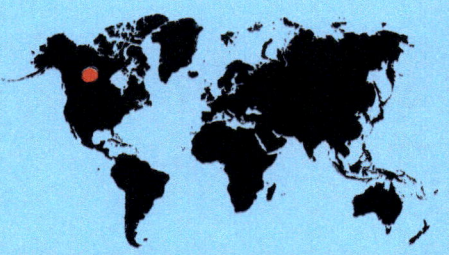

Maple Syrup: The Sweet Gold of the North: In Canada, maple syrup isn't just for pancakes; it's a national treasure. They love it so much, they even have a strategic maple syrup reserve. That's right, while other countries store oil or gold, Canada has vats of syrup. It's like their plan for world domination involves making everything delicious.

The Friendly Canadians: Canadians are famous for being polite. It's almost a national sport. Don't be surprised if you bump into someone and they apologize to you. In Canada, saying "sorry" is like saying "hello," and sometimes, it's hard to tell the difference.

Land of the Giants: Canada loves big things – and we're not just talking about mountains and lakes. Across the country, you'll find giant roadside attractions, like a massive hockey stick, a huge dinosaur, and even a gigantic nickel. It's like Canada is collecting items for a giant's souvenir shop. Drive across the country, and you'll feel like you're on a scavenger hunt for giant knick-knacks!

CANARY ISLANDS
Spain

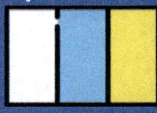

Atlantic Africa
population: 2,172,944
Size (sq miles): 2,893
Size (sq km): 7,493

The Islands of Eternal Spring: The Canary Islands are often called the "Islands of Eternal Spring" because of their fantastic year-round weather. It's like Mother Nature picked them as her favorite vacation spot. Here, winter jackets are as rare as a bad day at the beach. You can literally forget what season it is – but who's complaining?

A Language That Whistles, Not Talks: On La Gomera, one of the smaller islands, there's a language called Silbo Gomero that's made entirely of whistles. Yes, you read that right – whistles! It was traditionally used to communicate across the island's steep valleys. It's like having a conversation with a bird, but with more gossip.

Lunar Landscapes in Lanzarote: Visit Lanzarote, and you might think you've landed on the moon. The island's volcanic landscapes are so otherworldly that astronauts trained here during the Apollo missions. Exploring its black sand beaches and lava fields is like being on a space adventure, minus the zero gravity. Just remember, no moonwalks required!

CAYMAN ISLANDS
United Kingdom

Carribbean
population: 81,546
Size (sq miles): 100
Size (sq km): 259

Stingray City - Where Rays Play Host: In the Cayman Islands, you can visit Stingray City, a shallow sandbar where friendly stingrays swim right up to you. It's like attending a sea party where stingrays are the hosts. They're so used to humans, they might just photobomb your underwater selfie!

Underwater Art Gallery: The Cayman Islands are home to an underwater sculpture park, created by artist Jason deCaires Taylor. It's like an art museum, but you'll need a snorkel instead of a ticket. These sculptures aren't just cool to look at; they also serve as artificial reefs. It's where art meets marine conservation, and fish are the critics.

Pirate Week Festival - Ahoy, Matey!: Every November, the Cayman Islands host a Pirate Week Festival. It's a week-long celebration with mock pirate invasions, treasure hunts, and parades. It's like Halloween, but with more eye patches and parrots. Don't be surprised if someone tries to recruit you into their pirate crew – it's all part of the fun!

CENTRAL AFRICAN REPUBLIC

Central Africa
population: 5,552,228
Size (sq miles): 240,535
Size (sq km):   622,984

A River Runs Through It - The Ubangi: The Central African Republic (CAR) is sliced in half by the Ubangi River, one of Africa's major rivers. It's like the country's own natural highway, except with more hippos and fewer toll booths. This river isn't just a pretty sight; it's the lifeline of the nation, bustling with boats and teeming with life.

Music - The Heartbeat of the Nation: In the CAR, music isn't just entertainment; it's a way of life. Traditional music here is rich and varied, with instruments like the balafon and ngombi harp. It's like each instrument has its own story to tell, and together, they create the soundtrack of the country. Whether it's a joyous celebration or a solemn moment, there's always a song to accompany it.

Vibrant Markets - The Colorful Chaos: The markets in the CAR are a sensory overload in the best possible way. They're bustling, vibrant, and colorful, offering everything from handmade crafts to fresh produce. It's like a carnival of commerce, where haggling is the main event. Navigating these markets is an adventure in itself – just remember where you entered, or you might end up with an unplanned extended tour!

CHAD

Central Africa
population: 18,523,165
Size (sq miles): 496,000
Size (sq km): 1,284,000

Lake Chad: The Shapeshifting Lake: Lake Chad is quite the magician. Once one of the largest lakes in the world, it has dramatically shrunk and grown over the years. It's like the lake can't decide on its size, much like someone trying on clothes in a fitting room. This aquatic chameleon provides livelihoods, food, and water to millions, proving it's more than just a body of water with an identity crisis.

Stargazing Like Nowhere Else: In the heart of the Sahara Desert, the Zakouma National Park offers one of the most stunning night skies you'll ever see. With minimal light pollution, it's like a planetarium, but Mother Nature runs the show. The stars aren't just twinkling dots here; they're like celestial fireworks celebrating the vastness of the universe.

Vibrant Markets That Buzz With Life: Chad's markets are bustling epicenters of culture and commerce. From N'Djamena's Grand Marché to smaller town bazaars, these markets are like a lively dance of colors, sounds, and smells. You can find everything from handmade crafts to local delicacies. It's like a treasure hunt, except the treasure is discovering new foods and artifacts. Just remember, haggling is part of the fun – it's almost a local sport!

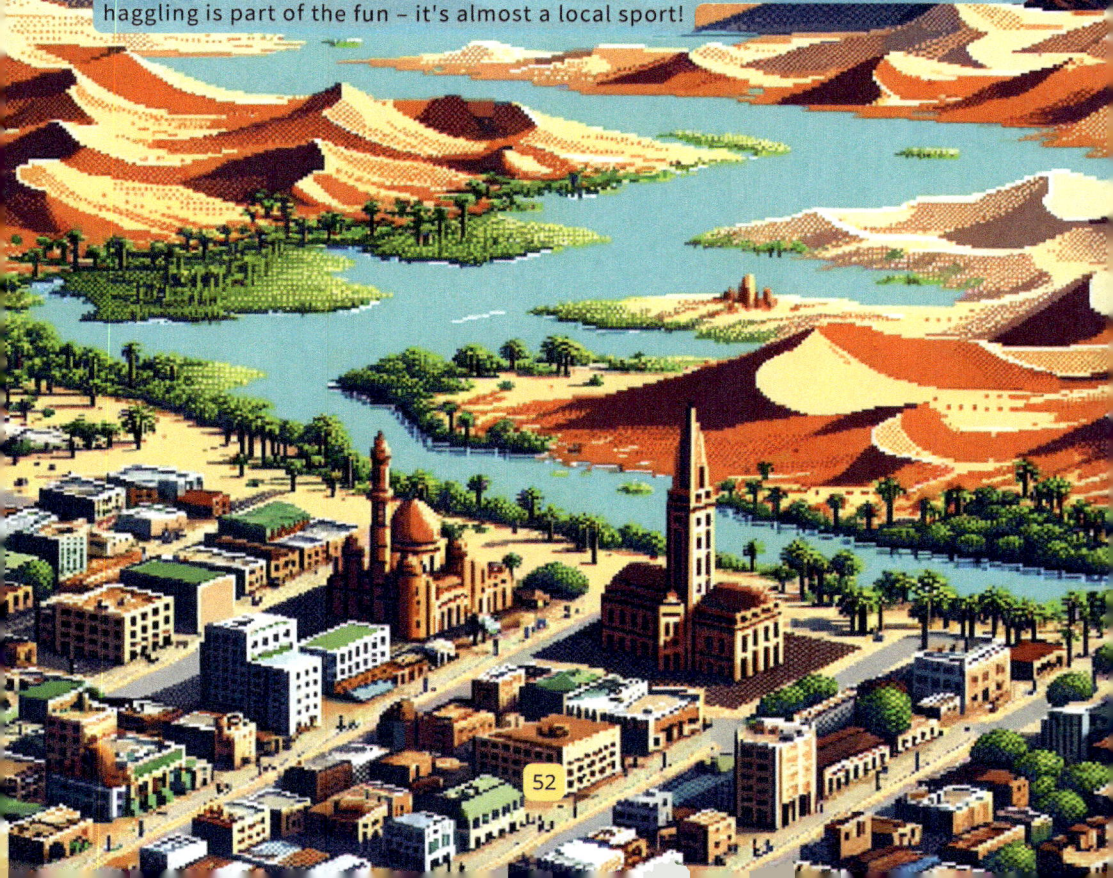

CHILE

South America
population: 19,629,588
Size (sq miles): 291,932.60
Size (sq km):   756,101.96

Stretching the Limits: The Long and Narrow Country: Chile is famously long and skinny. It stretches over 4,300 kilometers from north to south but is only about 177 kilometers wide. This means you could be skiing in the Andes and, within a few hours, be surfing in the Pacific Ocean. It's like Chile is trying to win a record for the world's most elongated country – talk about stretching yourself thin!

Poetry in the Air: The Land of Nobel Laureates: Chile is not just about stunning landscapes; it's also a land of poets. Two of its residents, Pablo Neruda and Gabriela Mistral, have won Nobel Prizes in Literature. Visiting Neruda's whimsically designed houses is like stepping into a poem itself. In Chile, it seems even the air whispers verses.

Cueca: The Dance of the Handkerchief: In Chile, the national dance, Cueca, involves a colorful handkerchief and some fancy footwork. It's a flirtatious dance mimicking a courting ritual between a rooster and a hen. Cueca is as fun as it sounds – dancers twirl and stomp, all while trying not to drop their handkerchiefs. It's like a game of 'how to impress your partner without tripping over your own feet.'

CHINA

East Asia
population: 1,409,670,000
Size (sq miles): 3,705,407
Size (sq km):   9,596,961

The Great Wall: China's Longest Landmark: The Great Wall of China is so long, it's like someone told the builders, "Just keep going until you hit the sea." Stretching over 21,000 kilometers, it's the only man-made structure visible from space. It's like ancient China's version of a 'No Trespassing' sign, but on a really grand scale.

Pandas: The Chubby Celebrities of China: In China, giant pandas are more than just cute faces; they're national treasures. Chengdu's Giant Panda Breeding Research Base lets you see these adorable creatures up close, munching on bamboo or just being their clumsy, cuddly selves. It's like a live version of your favorite panda video, only better because there's no loading time.

The Spring Festival: A Celebration with a Bang: Chinese New Year, or the Spring Festival, isn't just a holiday; it's the mother of all celebrations. It's marked with fireworks, dragon dances, and family feasts. Red envelopes with money are given for good luck – it's like Halloween for your wallet. During this festival, China turns into a riot of colors and sounds, proving that when it comes to celebrating, they don't do things by halves.

COLOMBIA

South America
population: 52,085,170
Size (sq miles): 440,831
Size (sq km): 1,141,748

Coffee So Good, It Deserves Its Own Zone: Colombia is renowned for its coffee, and it takes its beans so seriously that there's an entire region named the Coffee Triangle. Here, coffee is not just a drink; it's a lifestyle. The coffee is so good, you might start wondering if they sprinkle a bit of magic in every cup. It's like the espresso shot you never knew you needed, every hour, on the hour.

Salsa Dancing: Where Feet Move Faster Than Thoughts: In Colombia, salsa is not just a type of dance; it's a national obsession. Cities like Cali are known as the world's salsa capitals, where people's feet move at lightning speed. It's like the dance floors are on fire and the only way to put it out is by dancing. Even if you have two left feet, in Colombia, you'll be salsa-ing in no time!

Cartagena: A Rainbow of Houses and History: Walking through the streets of Cartagena is like strolling through a box of crayons. The city is famous for its colorful colonial buildings and vibrant street life. It's a place where every wall has a story, and every corner is a photo opportunity. It's like the buildings got dressed up in their favorite colors just to make your day brighter.

COMOROS

Africa - Indian Ocean
population: 850,886
Size (sq miles): 863
Size (sq km):   2,235

Mount Karthala: The Sleepy Giant: On the island of Grande Comore lies Mount Karthala, one of the world's largest active volcanoes. It's like the island's own moody teenager – mostly calm, but occasionally having a bit of an outburst. Hiking up this giant is an adventure; just make sure it's not having a 'grumpy' day!

The Perfume Isles: Where Scents Fill the Air: Comoros is known as the 'Perfume Isles' for its aromatic production of ylang-ylang, vanilla, and cloves. The air here smells like nature's own boutique perfume shop. It's like the islands decided to compete with your favorite fragrance – and they're winning.

Moonlit Beaches: The Natural Nightlight: The beaches in Comoros have a special charm at night, especially under a full moon. The moonlight reflecting on the water turns the beaches into a scene from a romantic movie. It's like the moon decided to show off, and the ocean's playing along. Walking along these beaches at night is a must-do – just remember, it's not a dream, it's Comoros!

CONGO-BRAZZAVILLE

Central Africa
population: 5,677,493
Size (sq miles): 132,000
Size (sq km): 342,000

The Mighty Congo River – Nature's Own Superhighway: Congo-Brazzaville is home to the mighty Congo River, the second-longest river in Africa. It's so big, you might mistake it for a moving lake. This river is like the main road of the country, but without traffic lights and with more hippos and crocodiles.

Music: The Heartbeat of the Nation: In Congo-Brazzaville, music isn't just background noise; it's a way of life. The country is a hotspot for rumba and soukous music, with beats so catchy, your feet start moving on their own. It's like the whole country is in a perpetual dance-off, and everyone's invited.

Sapeurs: The Dandies of Brazzaville: The Sapeurs, members of the Société des Ambianceurs et des Personnes Élégantes (Society of Tastemakers and Elegant People), take fashion to another level. These gentlemen dress in colorful, stylish outfits that could outshine a peacock. Walking down the streets, they turn everyday life into a fashion runway. It's like a daily 'who's the snazziest' contest, and the whole city's a judge.

COOK ISLANDS

Oceania · South Pacific
population: 15,040
Size (sq miles): 91.4
Size (sq km): 236.7

A Constellation of Islands: The Cook Islands are like a sprinkle of 15 tiny gems across the vast Pacific Ocean. Each island has its own personality – from the buzzing markets of Rarotonga to the untouched beauty of Aitutaki. It's like Mother Nature played a game of 'island scatter' and ended up creating a paradise.

Stargazing: A Celestial Spectacle: With little light pollution, the night skies in the Cook Islands are a stargazer's dream. The stars twinkle like a disco ball, and if you're lucky, you might catch the mesmerizing dance of the Southern Lights. It's like the universe decided to put on a nightly light show, just for you.

Coconut Wireless – The Island's News Network: Forget internet and 5G; in the Cook Islands, 'coconut wireless' is how news travels. It's the gossip grapevine, island style. Information passes from one person to another like a game of telephone, but with more coconuts and less miscommunication. It's not just a way to stay informed; it's a way to stay connected. Just remember, on the coconut wireless, every day is breaking news day!

COSTA RICA

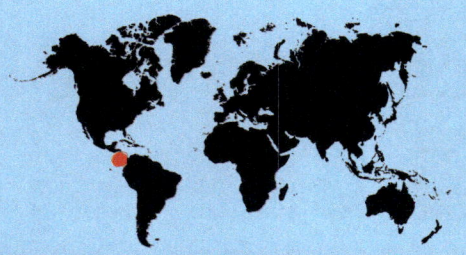

Central America
population: 5,044,197
Size (sq miles): 19,700
Size (sq km):   51,100

Pura Vida – More Than Just a Phrase: In Costa Rica, 'Pura Vida' is the mantra. It means 'pure life,' but it's more than that – it's a way of life. Used as a greeting, a farewell, or just when you're feeling good, it embodies the relaxed and happy lifestyle. In Costa Rica, even the clocks seem to be on Pura Vida time, moving just a bit slower.

The Rainforest Skywalks: Costa Rica's rainforests are stunning, but have you ever seen them from above? The country boasts several hanging bridges, offering a bird's-eye view of the forest. It's like walking through the treetops, but with less Tarzan-style swinging and more "oohs" and "aahs" at the incredible views.

Sloths: The Adorable Ambassadors: If Costa Rica had a mascot, it would be the sloth. These slow-moving creatures are the stars of the rainforest, winning hearts with their leisurely lifestyle and permanent smiles. Spotting a sloth is like finding a slow-moving, furry treasure – just don't hold your breath for them to do anything quickly. They're the living embodiment of the Pura Vida spirit!

CÔTE D'IVOIRE

West Africa
population: 29,344,847
Size (sq miles): 124,504
Size (sq km):   322,463

The Sweet Side of Côte d'Ivoire - World's Top Cocoa Producer: Love chocolate? Thank Côte d'Ivoire! This West African nation is the world's largest producer of cocoa, the main ingredient in chocolate. It's like the country is the global headquarters for chocoholics. Imagine if their rivers flowed with chocolate – Willy Wonka would have some serious competition!

The Fabric of Life - Vibrant and Colorful: In Côte d'Ivoire, traditional clothing is an explosion of color and pattern. The most famous fabric is the 'pagne', used in all sorts of garments, from everyday wear to ceremonial dress. Wearing these clothes is like carrying a piece of art – but more wearable and less likely to get you in trouble at the museum.

The Beat Goes On - Zaouli Dance and Mask Tradition: The Zaouli dance and mask tradition is a mesmerizing spectacle combining rhythm, dance, and elaborate masks. Each mask, brightly colored and intricately designed, represents different deities and spirits. Watching the Zaouli dance is like being in a trance – except you're allowed to move your feet and join in the fun!

CROATIA

Europe · Balkans
population: 3,855,641
Size (sq miles): 21,851
Size (sq km):   56,594

The Dalmatian Coast: Not Just About Spotted Dogs: Croatia's Dalmatian Coast is like the supermodel of seashores – long, stunning, and photogenic. With over 1,000 islands, it's a sailor's paradise and a beach lover's dream. And no, despite the name, you won't find any spotted dogs running the show, but you will find clear blue waters and picturesque towns.

The Genius of Nikola Tesla, A Croatian Star: Did you know Nikola Tesla, the wizard of electrical engineering, was born in Croatia? This land doesn't just have scenic views; it also produces brilliant minds. It's like there's something in the water (or maybe the Rakija) that breeds inventiveness.

Dubrovnik: A Real-Life King's Landing: Fans of "Game of Thrones" will recognize Dubrovnik as the stand-in for King's Landing. Walking through its old town is like stepping onto a medieval movie set, except the dragons are replaced by throngs of tourists, and the only thing you're likely to battle is a selfie stick. Dubrovnik's walls have seen centuries of history, and now they've seen dragons – well, at least in CGI.

CUBA

Carribbean
population: 10,985,974
Size (sq miles): 42,800
Size (sq km):   110,860

Time-Travel with Vintage Cars: In Cuba, it's like time travel is possible, at least when it comes to cars. The streets are filled with vibrant, vintage American cars from the 1950s. It's as if the cars decided they loved Cuba so much, they simply refused to age. Riding in one is like starring in your own classic movie, with a tropical twist.

Salsa: In Cuba, salsa music and dancing are part of the soul of the country. It's not just in dance halls and clubs, but in the streets, homes, and even the occasional plaza. The rhythm is so infectious, you might find your hips moving before your brain gives permission. It's like the entire island is swaying to a beat that says, "Life is a dance, join in!"

Beaches as Sweet as Sugar: Cuba's beaches are famous for their sugar-white sands and crystal-clear waters. Places like Varadero Beach offer a slice of paradise where the sand is as fine as powdered sugar (but please, no taste testing). Lounging on a Cuban beach is like being in a postcard, except the breeze and the sound of the waves are real.

CURAÇAO
The Netherlands

Carribbean
population: 148,925
Size (sq miles): 171
Size (sq km): 444

Willemstad: Where Buildings are a Paint Palette: In Curaçao's capital, Willemstad, the buildings look like they've been dipped in a rainbow. Legend has it that a former governor ordered them painted in bright colors to ease his headache from the sun's reflection on white walls. Whether that's true or not, the result is a cityscape that looks like a box of crayons had a party – and everyone's invited.

Diving into an Underwater Wonderland: Curaçao isn't just beautiful above water; below the surface, it's a kaleidoscope of marine life. The island boasts some of the best diving spots, with coral reefs, sunken ships, and an underwater sculpture park. It's like entering a different world where fish are the locals, and you're the curious tourist.

Papiamentu – The Language Cocktail: The local language, Papiamentu, is a linguistic smoothie blending Dutch, Spanish, Portuguese, and African languages. In Curaçao, saying hello can be a mini language lesson. It's like the islanders couldn't decide on a language, so they chose all of them. Speaking Papiamentu is like attending a family reunion with words from all over the world.

CYPRUS

Middle East
population: 1,244,188
Size (sq miles): 3,572
Size (sq km): 9,251

Aphrodite's Birthplace: Where Beauty Begins: According to legend, Cyprus is the birthplace of Aphrodite, the Greek goddess of love and beauty. The famous rock, Petra tou Romiou, is where she's said to have emerged from the sea. It's like the island is the original beauty queen, giving everyone else a run for their money. Don't forget to snap a selfie with Aphrodite's rock – it's like ancient Greece's version of a celebrity photo op!

Halloumi: More Than Just Cheese: In Cyprus, halloumi isn't just a cheese; it's a national treasure. This squeaky, salty delight is found in almost every meal – grilled, fried, or fresh. It's like the Swiss Army knife of cheeses, versatile and ready for any culinary challenge. Halloumi is to Cypriots what pizza is to Italians – essential and delicious.

Cats, Cats, and More Cats: Cyprus is home to many cats, so much so that they're part of local folklore. Legend has it that Saint Helena imported cats to control snakes. Today, these furry residents are as much a part of the island as the sunny beaches. It's like living in a paradise tailored for cat lovers – where every alley and corner has a feline friend ready to welcome (or ignore) you.

CZECHIA

Central Europe
population: 10,827,529
Size (sq miles): 30,452
Size (sq km): 78,871

Castles Straight Out of a Fairy Tale: Czechia could easily be the backdrop for any fairy tale with its over 2,000 castles and chateaux – the highest density in the world! It's like the country won a contest for who could build the most castles, and then just kept going. From the grandeur of Prague Castle to the charm of Český Krumlov, each castle has its own story, minus the dragons and damsels in distress.

Puppetry: In Czechia, puppetry isn't just child's play; it's serious art. With a tradition dating back centuries, Czech puppet shows are a blend of craftsmanship, storytelling, and humor. It's where wooden characters come to life, and not just in a Pinocchio kind of way. Attending a puppet show in Czechia is like stepping into a whimsical world where strings definitely come attached.

Beer: More Than a Beverage: Czechs love their beer – so much so that they're the top beer drinkers in the world per capita. Beer is not just a drink here; it's a national hobby. From classic pilsners to craft brews, beer in Czechia is like water elsewhere, except tastier and with a bit more cheer. Don't be surprised if 'going for a coffee' turns into grabbing a pint.

DEMOCRATIC REPUBLIC OF THE CONGO

Central Africa
population: 111,859,928
Size (sq miles): 905,567
Size (sq km):   2,345,409

The Congo River - Africa's Mighty Waterway: In the Democratic Republic of the Congo (DRC), the Congo River is so massive it's like the country's main highway, except with more water and fewer road signs. This river is the second-largest in Africa and is the lifeline for transportation and livelihoods. It's so big, you might start wondering if it's trying to compete with the ocean.

Rumba: The Rhythm of the Streets: In the DRC, music is a big deal, especially Congolese rumba. It's not just a genre; it's the heartbeat of the nation. The streets buzz with music, from makeshift drum sets and thumb pianos. It's like the entire country is a dance floor, and everyone's invited to show off their moves.

Home to the Elusive Okapi: The DRC is one of the only places in the world where you can find the okapi, a unique animal that looks like a zebra got mixed up with a giraffe. These shy creatures are exclusive to the Congolese rainforest, making them celebrities in the animal kingdom. Spotting an okapi in the wild is like winning a nature lottery – rare but thrilling!

DENMARK

Europe · Scandinavia
population: 5,935,619
Size (sq miles): 16,639
Size (sq km):   43,094

Mastering the Art of Coziness with 'Hygge': In Denmark, 'hygge' (pronounced 'hoo-ga') is the way of life. It's all about coziness, comfort, and contentment. Think warm blankets, candlelight, and good company. It's like the Danes found a way to bottle up the feeling of a warm hug and spread it everywhere. In Denmark, even the coldest, darkest winter days have a warm, fuzzy side.

Home to Hans Christian Andersen's Fairy Tales: Wander through the streets of Copenhagen, and you might feel like you've stepped into a fairy tale. This is, after all, the land of Hans Christian Andersen. Visit the Little Mermaid statue, inspired by his famous tale, but don't be shocked by her size – she's famously smaller than most expect. It's like she's saying, "Good things come in small packages."

Biking: More Than a Mode of Transport: In Denmark, bicycles are king. There are more bikes than cars, making it a cyclist's paradise. It's like everyone chose two wheels over four, and traffic jams are more about bell ringing than horn honking. Cycling in Denmark is not just a way to get around; it's a national pastime and, for many, the favorite way to enjoy the Danish scenery – wind in your hair and all.

DJIBOUTI

East Africa
population: 976,143
Size (sq miles): 8,958
Size (sq km):   23,200

Lake Assal: A Salt Lake Below Sea Level: Djibouti is home to Lake Assal, the lowest point in Africa and one of the saltiest bodies of water in the world. It's like nature's own salt shaker, but way bigger. The lake is so salty, you can float in it effortlessly – it's like the Dead Sea's lesser-known cousin who loves to show off its buoyancy skills.

The Underwater Kaleidoscope of the Red Sea: Off the coast of Djibouti, the Red Sea offers some of the most spectacular diving spots. It's like a giant, natural aquarium where the fish are always ready for a close-up, and the corals think they're in a beauty contest. Diving here is like entering a different world, one where sharks are friendly locals, not movie villains.

Tea Time is Any Time: In Djibouti, tea isn't just a drink; it's a ritual. Whether it's first thing in the morning or late in the evening, there's always time for tea. It's like the universal answer to all of life's questions. Stressed? Have some tea. Happy? Celebrate with tea. Tired? Tea will fix it. It's the warm, comforting hug in a cup that everyone loves.

DOMINICA

Carribbean
population: 72,412
Size (sq miles): 290
Size (sq km):   750

Boiling Lake: Nature's Own Cauldron: Dominica hosts one of the world's few boiling lakes, and it's exactly what it sounds like – a lake that's literally boiling! Nestled in Morne Trois Pitons National Park, this geothermal wonder is like nature's hot tub, except you definitely don't want to take a dip. The journey there is a hike through a lush rainforest, like a quest to find a mystical, steamy brew.

Whale Watching: In the waters around Dominica, you can spot sperm whales, making it a premier destination for whale watchers. It's like the whales are putting on a show, and everyone's invited – no binoculars needed. The whales are so regular, they're like the friendly neighbors you see every day, only bigger and with flippers.

Jump-Up Creole Music Festivals: Dominica's music scene is vibrant with its unique Creole music, a lively blend of African, European, and indigenous influences. The World Creole Music Festival is a highlight, where locals and visitors alike dance to the pulsating rhythms. It's like the island turns into one big dance floor, and the beat is so infectious, even the shyest feet find themselves tapping along.

DOMINICAN REPUBLIC

Carribbean
population: 11,434,005
Size (sq miles): 18,792
Size (sq km): 48,671

Beaches That Look Like Phone Backgrounds: The Dominican Republic is famous for its postcard-worthy beaches, with crystal-clear waters and soft, white sands. It's like someone used a filter to enhance the colors, but nope, that's just their everyday scenery. These beaches are so perfect, you'll start doubting whether you're awake or still dreaming about your vacation plans.

Baseball: More Than a Game: In the Dominican Republic, baseball isn't just a sport; it's a way of life. The island has produced more MLB players than any other country outside the U.S. It's like every kid grows up with a baseball glove in one hand and dreams of grand slams in their eyes. Here, 'home run' is a common phrase, both on and off the field.

Merengue: The Rhythm That Moves a Nation: Dominican Republic is the birthplace of merengue, a fast-paced, hip-swinging music and dance that's at the heart of every party. It's so infectious; you'll find yourself moving to the beat even if you've got two left feet. Merengue is like the island's heartbeat, audible at every street corner, bringing everyone together in a dance of joy.

ECUADOR

South America
population: 17,483,326
Size (sq miles): 109,484
Size (sq km): 283,561

Straddling the Equator - Middle of the World: Ecuador is one of the few countries in the world lucky enough to be bisected by the equator. It's home to the "Mitad del Mundo" monument, where you can stand with one foot in each hemisphere. It's like doing a global split without the gymnastics – a perfect photo op to show you're in two places at once!

Galápagos Islands: Darwin's Playground: The Galápagos Islands, part of Ecuador, are where Charles Darwin got his big ideas about evolution. It's a unique showcase of wildlife, where the animals seem to have missed the memo on human fear. Here, you can meet giant tortoises, playful sea lions, and birds that don't mind a selfie or two. It's like walking into a live nature documentary.

Panama Hats: Actually Made in Ecuador: Contrary to their name, Panama hats originated in Ecuador. These straw hats are handwoven and were historically exported via Panama, hence the mix-up. Wearing one is not just about style; it's like donning a piece of history and culture – with the added bonus of sun protection!

EGYPT

North Africa
population: 110,000,000
Size (sq miles): 390,121
Size (sq km):   1,010,408

The Pyramids: Egypt's Eternal Triangles: Egypt is famous for its pyramids, especially the Great Pyramid of Giza, one of the Seven Wonders of the Ancient World. These monumental tombs were built without modern machinery, which makes you wonder if the ancient Egyptians knew something we don't. Visiting them is like stepping into a time machine, except the only button is 'way back'.

The Sphinx: A Cat with a Riddle: The Great Sphinx of Giza is one of the most mysterious monuments in Egypt. It's a lion's body with a human head – kind of like an ancient Egyptian version of Photoshop. There are many theories about its nose missing, from Napoleon's soldiers using it for target practice to just really bad erosion. It's the ultimate 'noseless' riddle.

Papyrus: The Ancient Paper Trail: Long before paper and emails, there was papyrus. This ancient form of paper was made from the papyrus plant found along the Nile Delta. It's like the Egyptians invented the first kind of notebook, but with more reeds and less Wi-Fi. Seeing papyrus being made is like watching a history lesson unfold before your eyes – one that you can actually take home and write on!

EL SALVADOR

Central America
population: 6,602,370
Size (sq miles): 8,124
Size (sq km): 21,041

Volcanoes Galore: Not Just a Pretty Peak: El Salvador is known as the 'Land of Volcanoes,' with over 20 of them dotting the landscape. It's like the country won a volcanic lottery. These natural wonders are not just for show – many are still active, offering hot springs and stunning views. Hiking here is like walking on a geological wonder, just with less lava than you might expect.

Pupusas: The Stuffed Delight: In El Salvador, pupusas are a big deal. These delicious stuffed tortillas are the national dish and for a good reason. Filled with cheese, beans, or meat, they're like the Salvadoran answer to pizza, but rounder, flatter, and arguably tastier. Eating pupusas is a hands-on experience – literally, as they're best enjoyed with your fingers!

Festivals of Color and Joy: El Salvador loves a good fiesta. The August Festival, celebrating the country's patron saint, is a burst of color, music, and dance. It's like the entire country turns into a party, and everyone's on the guest list. These festivals are a vibrant display of Salvadoran culture – think Mardi Gras, but with more pupusas and less beads.

ENGLAND
United Kingdom

Western Europe
population: 56,536,419
Size (sq miles): 51,320
Size (sq km):   132,938

The Queen's Guards: Stoic and Bearskin-Clad: When you're in England, don't miss the Queen's Guards, famous for their red coats and tall bearskin hats. These guards are so good at standing still, you might mistake them for statues – until they blink. And remember, no matter how funny your jokes are, these guys won't crack a smile. It's like a real-life version of the "try not to laugh" challenge.

Big Ben: More Than Just a Clock: Big Ben is one of England's most iconic landmarks, but here's a fun fact: Big Ben is actually the name of the bell, not the clock or the tower. It's like finding out Santa Claus' real name is Jeff. Standing tall and timely, this clock has been keeping Londoners punctual since 1859 – give or take a few maintenance breaks.

Tea Time: A National Sport: In England, tea is more than a beverage; it's a ritual. It's like the country collectively decided that every problem could be at least contemplated, if not solved, over a cup of tea. Whether it's morning, noon, or night, there's always time for tea – and maybe a biscuit or two. Just remember, tea time is a serious affair – but pinkies up is optional.

EQUATORIAL GUINEA

Central Africa
population: 1,679,172
Size (sq miles): 10,830
Size (sq km): 28,050

Island Hopping with a Twist: Equatorial Guinea is one of the only countries in Africa with an island capital – Malabo, located on Bioko Island. It's like the country decided to put its capital on vacation mode. Exploring Bioko Island offers a mix of beautiful beaches, volcanic views, and a capital city with a unique island vibe. It's island life with a presidential twist.

Spanish Flavor in Africa: As a former Spanish colony, Equatorial Guinea is the only country in Africa where Spanish is an official language. Strolling through the streets of Malabo, you'll encounter Spanish colonial architecture, giving you a feeling of being in two continents at once. It's like Spain and Africa had a baby, and they named it Equatorial Guinea.

Football: The Unofficial National Language: In Equatorial Guinea, football (soccer) isn't just a sport; it's a passion. The national team, known as the Nzalang Nacional, brings the country together like a good family drama. Watching a match is like attending a national festival where every goal scored is a reason for a nationwide celebration. It's the one time when everyone speaks the same language – football!

ERITREA

East Africa
population: 6,700,000
Size (sq miles): 45,400
Size (sq km):   117,600

Asmara - A City Frozen in Time: Asmara, the capital of Eritrea, is like a living museum of Italian Art Deco architecture. It's as if the city decided to throw a 1930s Italian-themed party and then never stopped. Strolling through Asmara, with its vintage Italian-style cafes and buildings, you might just feel like asking for a cappuccino in your best Italian accent.

Cycling is Almost a National Sport: Eritreans love cycling – it's huge here! It's like the Tour de France, but on Eritrean streets, and every day is race day. The country has produced some top-notch cyclists, so don't be surprised if you're overtaken by someone who looks like they're training for the Olympics – they just might be!

The Art of Coffee Making: In Eritrea, coffee isn't just a drink; it's an event. The traditional coffee ceremony is an elaborate process involving roasting, grinding, and brewing, usually done in beautiful attire. It's like attending a coffee opera, where the aroma fills the air and each sip tells a story. Participating in this ceremony is like being knighted in the ancient order of caffeine lovers.

ESTONIA

Eastern Europe
population: 1,373,101
Size (sq miles): 17,505
Size (sq km): 45,339

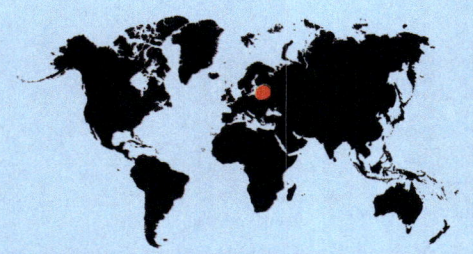

E-Estonia: The Country You Can Click Through: Estonia is so digitally advanced, it's like living in the future. They've got e-Residency, e-Voting, e-Healthcare – basically, an 'e-' before everything. It's like the whole country was developed by tech wizards. Here, you can vote in your pajamas, see a doctor on your laptop, and start a business faster than you can make a sandwich.

The Singing Nation: Estonia loves singing so much, they sang their way to freedom in the late 1980s, known as the Singing Revolution. Their national song festival, Laulupidu, is a massive choir event that can bring together over 30,000 singers. It's like the whole country decided to start a band, and everyone's invited. Just imagine the choir practice sessions!

Saaremaa: Home to Meteorite Craters and Quirky Windmills: Saaremaa, Estonia's largest island, is famous for its windmills and the Kaali crater, caused by a meteorite over 3,500 years ago. It's like the island is a magnet for wind and space rocks. Visiting Saaremaa is like stepping into a storybook where every chapter is more fascinating than the last.

ESWATINI

Southern Africa
population: 1,236,126
Size (sq miles): 6,704
Size (sq km): 17,364

Land of Rolling Hills and Friendly Wildlife: Eswatini, formerly known as Swaziland, is a tiny kingdom boasting stunning landscapes of rolling hills and mountains. It's like the country is wearing a crinkled green blanket, except this blanket is dotted with zebras and antelopes casually grazing. Hiking here is less about the exercise and more about who you might meet on the trail – and by meet, I mean the four-legged locals.

The Umhlanga Reed Dance: A Royal Affair: One of Eswatini's most famous events is the Umhlanga or Reed Dance, a vibrant cultural festival. Thousands of young women gather to perform for the King, carrying reeds to reinforce the windbreak around the royal residence. It's like a combination of a beauty pageant and a home improvement show, but with more dancing and singing.

Eswatini's Own Railway Museum: In a charming twist, Eswatini has a railway museum that celebrates its rail history. It's not quite the Orient Express, but it's full of old-timey charm. Exploring this museum is like chugging through the pages of a history book, except here, you can actually touch the exhibits and not get a stern look from a librarian.

ETHIOPIA

East Africa
population: 127,955,823
Size (sq miles): 429,000
Size (sq km): 1,112,000

The Cradle of Civilization and a Calendar Time Forgot: Ethiopia is often called the 'Cradle of Civilization' because it's where some of the oldest human remains were found. It's also the country that said, "Gregorian Calendar, who?" and kept its own, which means they're around seven years behind the rest of the world. In Ethiopia, time travel is real, at least on paper.

High-Altitude Running: A National Pastime: Ever wondered why Ethiopian athletes dominate long-distance running? Much of the country sits over 2,500 meters above sea level. Training at such altitudes, Ethiopians basically gain super lungs. It's like living in a natural, high-altitude training camp, but with more scenic views and less fancy gym equipment.

Coffee: Not Just a Drink, But a Ceremony: In Ethiopia, coffee isn't just a beverage; it's an elaborate ceremony. The process involves roasting beans, brewing them in a clay pot called a 'jebena,' and enjoying the drink with friends. It's like a coffee lover's dream ritual, where every sip is steeped in tradition and community. And let's face it, Ethiopian coffee could probably wake up a sleeping mountain.

FALKLAND ISLANDS
United Kingdom

South America - South Atlantic
population: 3,662
Size (sq miles): 4,700
Size (sq km):   12,173

Penguin Paradise: The Falkland Islands might as well be called "Penguin Kingdom." Home to five different species, including the rockhopper with its funky hairdo, it's like the penguins got together and declared it their favorite hangout spot. Here, you're more likely to bump into a penguin than another person. It's a waddle-fest where the penguins are the main attraction, and humans are just the paparazzi.

A Museum of Shipwrecks: The Falklands have more shipwrecks per square mile than anywhere else in the world. It's as if ships saw the islands and thought, "This seems like a nice place to retire." These rusting hulks aren't just eerie landmarks; they're like natural history museums that chose the ocean as their final exhibit space.

A Cup of Tea at the Edge of the World: Despite being way down in the South Atlantic, the Falkland Islands keep up the British tradition of teatime. It's like Britain said, "Here, have some remote islands and don't forget to bring the tea." Whether you're in the capital, Stanley, or a cozy countryside farm, there's always time for a cuppa, complete with biscuits and a chat about the weather.

FAROE ISLANDS
Denmark

Northern Europe
population: 54,557
Size (sq miles): 538
Size (sq km): 1,393

Cliffs That Sing and Roar: The Faroe Islands are a paradise for cliff enthusiasts (if that's a thing). With dramatic cliffs that plunge into the North Atlantic, the islands seem like they're auditioning for a role in a nature documentary. The wind here doesn't just howl; it sings in a full-blown choir with the waves providing the bass. It's wild up here, really wild...

Sheep Outnumber People: In the Faroe Islands, sheep are the unofficial rulers. They outnumber the human population and have the right of way on roads. It's like living in a woolly kingdom where traffic jams are caused by sheep deciding to have a meeting in the middle of the road. Just remember, in the Faroe Islands, 'sheepish' driving is the norm.

Houses with Grass Roofs: Many homes in the Faroe Islands come with their own natural green hats. These grass roofs aren't just charming; they're also great insulators. It's like the houses decided to go green in the most literal way. Plus, these roofs provide the perfect spot for local sheep to graze – because why eat at ground level when you can dine on a rooftop?

FIJI

Oceania
population: 926,276
Size (sq miles): 7,056
Size (sq km): 18,274

More Islands Than Days of the Year: Fiji is made up of about 333 islands, giving you one for almost every day of the year. It's like Fiji was playing a game of island bingo and just kept saying, "Yes, we'll take another one." Each island offers its own slice of paradise – from luxurious private isles to unspoiled natural beauties. Island hopping here could be a full-time job, and what a job that would be!

Fire-Walking: Not Just a Party Trick: In Fiji, the Sawau tribe on Beqa Island has a centuries-old tradition of fire-walking. It's not just a daring feat but a sacred ritual. Watching these brave souls walk calmly over hot stones is like witnessing a real-life magic act, except the only magic here is strong tradition and tougher feet.

The Bula Spirit: A Cheerful Welcome Everywhere: 'Bula' is the Fijian way of saying hello, and it's more than just a greeting; it's a show of happiness and friendliness. In Fiji, expect to hear "Bula!" accompanied by a wide smile almost everywhere you go. It's as if the entire nation attended a seminar on how to be the world's best hosts, and everyone graduated with flying colors. "Bula" isn't just a word; it's a warm Fijian hug in verbal form.

FINLAND

Europe · Scandinavia
population: 5,604,558
Size (sq miles): 130,559
Size (sq km):   338,145

Lake aplenty: In Finland, they say there's a lake for every day of the year – and then some. With over 188,000 lakes, it's like Finland won the lake lottery and decided to keep all the winnings. These lakes are so much a part of Finnish life, you might start wondering if 'lake' is just Finnish for 'backyard.'

Sauna: More Than Just a Hot Room: The Finns didn't just invent the sauna; they turned it into a national pastime. With over 2 million saunas, it's like every Finnish person is born with a sauna membership. It's a place for relaxation, socializing, and occasionally making important decisions – because why not discuss business or politics in a room where everyone's just wearing towels?

Home of Santa Claus: Yes, Santa Claus! According to Finnish lore, Santa lives in Korvatunturi, in Lapland. It's like the North Pole's back office, handling all the gift logistics. Visiting Finland, especially during winter, is like stepping into a Christmas card scene – complete with reindeer, but the elves are on break.

FRANCE

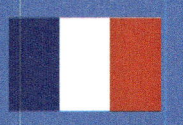

Western Europe
population: 68,373,433
Size (sq miles): 213,011
Size (sq km):   551,695

Eiffel Tower: More Than Just Metal: The Eiffel Tower, originally considered a temporary eyesore by some Parisians, is now one of the most famous structures in the world. It's like the ultimate Cinderella story, but with iron and elevators. And it's not just for looking at - every year, millions of people climb it just to say, "Oui, I did it!"

Cuisine: A Love Affair with Food: French cuisine is like an art form, where butter is the paint and the plate is the canvas. From croissants that make your morning brighter to cheese that deserves its own museum, the French take their food seriously. It's a place where even the snails are considered a delicacy - dressed in garlic and butter, of course.

The Louvre, a museum to rule them all: The Louvre isn't just a museum; it's a treasure trove of art and history. Yes, Mona Lisa lives here, with her enigmatic smile, but she shares her home with thousands of other masterpieces. Visiting the Louvre is like taking a walk through the annals of human creativity – but remember, it's so large, you might need breadcrumbs to find your way back out.

FRENCH GUIANA
France

South America
population: 295,385
Size (sq miles): 32,000
Size (sq km): 84,000

The Spaceport Next Door: French Guiana is home to the Guiana Space Centre, Europe's gateway to the stars. It's like having NASA as your next-door neighbor, except with more croissants and less gravity. Watching a rocket launch here is like seeing science fiction come to life, just without the aliens (as far as we know).

Rainforests and Rivers Galore: Over 90% of French Guiana is covered in dense, lush rainforests. It's like Mother Nature decided to go wild with the green paint. These forests are teeming with wildlife, from colorful birds to chatty monkeys, and rivers that look like they've been lifted from a travel magazine. Exploring here is like stepping into a real-life adventure novel.

Carnival: A Festival of Colors and Costumes: French Guiana's Carnival is one of the most vibrant in the Americas. It's a time when the streets burst into life with music, dance, and costumes that would make a peacock jealous. This carnival is not just a party; it's a full-blown extravaganza where everyone is invited to dance, sing, and forget about their worries - until the music stops.

FRENCH POLYNESIA

France

Oceania
population: 278,786
Size (sq miles): 1,609
Size (sq km):   4,167

The Overwater Bungalow: Sleep on the Sea: French Polynesia is famous for its dreamy overwater bungalows. It's like someone thought, "Why stay beside the water when you can stay right on top of it?" These bungalows offer a unique sleeping experience where the ocean is literally under your bed. It's the only place where you might need a lifejacket as a bedside accessory.

Tattoos: More Than Just Skin Deep: In French Polynesia, tattoos are a big deal. They're not just body art; they're storytelling. Each design symbolizes a person's life, beliefs, and social status. It's like wearing your diary on your skin, but way cooler and with less risk of someone reading it over your shoulder.

The Tamure: Dance Like Everyone's Watching: The tamure is the traditional dance of French Polynesia, known for its fast hip-shaking moves to the beats of drums. It's like Zumba, but with more grass skirts and less gym attire. Attending a tamure performance or joining in is a must – it's the perfect way to shake off any excess energy, or just show off your killer dance moves.

GABON

Central Africa
population: 2,397,368
Size (sq miles): 103,347
Size (sq km): 267,668

A Jungle So Dense, Even the Sun Needs a GPS: Gabon is a paradise for nature lovers, with over 80% of its land covered in rainforests. These aren't just any forests; they're so dense and lush, you might expect Tarzan to swing by at any moment. Trekking through Gabon's jungles is like stepping into a green wonderland, where every leaf and vine has a story to tell.

Surf's Up, Hippos!: In Gabon's Loango National Park, you might catch hippos doing something unusual – surfing! Yes, these hefty herbivores love to ride the waves. It's like they saw the surfers and thought, "That looks fun, let's give it a try." Watching a hippo catch a wave is like seeing a ballet dancer do a breakdance – unexpected but oddly graceful.

Masks More Than a Fashion Statement: In Gabon, masks aren't just for ceremonies; they're a living art. Each mask tells a story, representing spirits, ancestors, or even social satire. During traditional dances, these masks come to life, moving to the rhythm of drums. It's like Halloween, but with deeper meaning and better dance moves.

GAMBIA

West Africa
population: 2,468,569
Size (sq miles): 4,400
Size (sq km):   11,300

The Gambia River: The Country's Lifeline: Gambia is unique because it's almost entirely enveloped by another country, except for its small Atlantic coastline. At its heart flows the mighty Gambia River, the country's main artery. It's like Gambia decided to be a country in the shape of a river – slender, winding, and full of life. Travel along it, and you're basically traversing the entire nation, no GPS needed!

The Smiling Coast of Africa: Gambia is often called the "Smiling Coast of Africa", and it's not just because of the shape of its coastline. Gambians are known for their warmth and hospitality. Visit Gambia, and you're guaranteed smiles wider than the river itself. It's like the whole country participated in a 'who can smile the widest' contest and everyone won.

Wrestling: In Gambia, wrestling is not just a sport; it's a cultural event, complete with music, dancing, and vibrant costumes. It's like a mix between a dance-off and a friendly tussle in the sand. Attending a wrestling match is like going to a party where the guests occasionally grapple – all in good spirit, of course.

GEORGIA

West Asia • Caucasus
population: 3,688,647
Size (sq miles): 26,900
Size (sq km): 69,700

Birthplace of Wine: Cheers to 8,000 Vintages!: Sorry France, Georgia claims to be the birthplace of wine, with a winemaking history stretching back over 8,000 years. It's like the country started the whole grape-to-glass trend before it was cool. Here, traditional wine is made in clay vessels called 'qvevri,' buried underground like a treasure – a very drinkable treasure.

The Caucasus Mountains: Europe's Dramatic Skyline: Georgia's northern border is framed by the towering Caucasus Mountains, offering postcard-worthy views and hiking adventures. It's like nature's own version of skyscrapers, but with more snow and less Wi-Fi. The peaks are so high, they seem to be having a conversation with the clouds.

Supra: The Feast Where Everyone's Family: A Georgian 'supra' is a traditional feast that's less about the food and more about the experience. It's hosted by a 'tamada' or toastmaster, who ensures the toasts keep coming, and so does the wine. Attending a supra is like joining a big, happy family dinner, where the word 'full' doesn't exist, and everyone becomes your 'cousin.' Just remember, in Georgia, leaving a supra hungry (or sober) is practically impossible.

GERMANY

Western Europe
population: 84,607,016
Size (sq miles): 138,100
Size (sq km):   357,600

Castles Right Out of a Storybook: Germany is sprinkled with castles so enchanting, you'd expect a fairy tale character to pop out at any moment. The most famous, Neuschwanstein Castle, inspired Disney's Sleeping Beauty castle. It's like Germany cornered the market on fairy tales, then built the castles to prove it. Just remember, dragons not included.

Bread Paradise - Over 300 Types!: In Germany, bread is not just a side dish; it's a cultural icon. With over 300 types of bread, German bakeries are like libraries, but for carbs. From crusty Brötchen to dense Pumpernickel, each bread is a masterpiece of baking art. Let's be honest, the real German engineering marvel might just be their bread ovens.

Efficiency: A Way of Life: The stereotype of German efficiency isn't just a stereotype. Trains that run on time, spotless streets, and a love for order are part of the national DNA. It's like Germany looked at the chaos of the world and said, "Nein, danke." This love for efficiency extends to their famous Autobahn – highways without speed limits in some parts, where even the fastest cars can feel like they're in the slow lane.

GHANA

West Africa
population: 34,237,628
Size (sq miles): 92,497
Size (sq km):   239,567

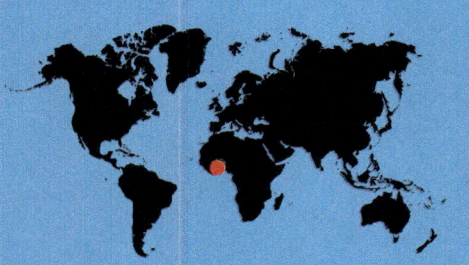

The Gold Coast with a Heart of Cocoa: Ghana, once known as the Gold Coast, is now world-famous for something just as rich – chocolate. As one of the largest cocoa producers, it's like the country swapped one kind of gold for another, equally delicious one. Here, chocolate isn't just a treat; it's a way of life. It's like finding Willy Wonka's factory, but in the heart of Africa.

Kente Cloth: More Than Just Fabric: In Ghana, the kente cloth is a symbol of pride and cultural identity. These brightly colored and intricately woven fabrics aren't just for wearing; they tell stories and signify status and heritage. Wearing kente is like donning a piece of history, except more stylish and with fewer dates to remember.

The Warmth of Ghanaian Hospitality: Ghanaians are known for their friendliness and hospitality. It's like the whole country has a 'mi casa es su casa' vibe. In Ghana, a stranger is just a friend you haven't shared a meal with yet. Don't be surprised if you're invited to join in a dance, a meal, or a conversation – it's just the Ghanaian way of saying, "Welcome!"

GIBRALTAR
United Kingdom

Southern Europe
population: 32,688
Size (sq miles): 2.6
Size (sq km):   6.8

The Rock of Gibraltar: The Rock of Gibraltar is not just any rock; it's a monolithic limestone promontory that stands guard at the gateway to the Mediterranean. It's like nature's own skyscraper, only with more monkeys and less office space. And speaking of monkeys...

Barbary Macaques: The Real Bosses of the Rock: Gibraltar is famous for its Barbary macaques, the only wild monkey population in Europe. They're cheeky, they're charming, and they firmly believe that what's yours is theirs – especially if it's edible. It's like visiting a wildlife park, but where the animals are in charge and the humans are on display.

A Melting Pot at the Crossroads: Located at the crossroads of Europe and Africa, Gibraltar is a melting pot of cultures, languages, and cuisines. It's British, but also Spanish, and a bit Moroccan, with a dash of its own unique flavor. Walking down its streets is like taking a mini Euro-African tour, only without the need for multiple visas. Just remember, in Gibraltar, you can have your fish and chips and eat your tapas too!

GREECE

Southern Europe
population: 10,413,982
Size (sq miles): 50,949
Size (sq km): 131,957

Ruins Older Than Your Great-Great-Grandma: In Greece, 'old' takes on a whole new meaning. With ancient ruins dating back thousands of years, it's like the country is the grandparent of Europe, telling stories of the past. The Parthenon, perched atop the Acropolis in Athens, is so old it makes medieval castles look like new builds. It's a place where history isn't just in textbooks; it's on every street corner, casually leaning against a coffee shop.

The Birthplace of the Olympics - and Marathons: Long before there were shiny medals and global broadcasts, Greece gave birth to the Olympic Games in 776 BC. It's like they invented the concept of "Go big or go home" in sports. And let's not forget the marathon, inspired by a legendary run from the Battle of Marathon to Athens. Nowadays, running 26.2 miles is a choice, not a battlefield necessity, thankfully.

Olives world: In Greece, olives aren't just something to put on pizza; they're a way of life. The country is one of the top olive producers, and the love for olives is evident. They're in the food, on the tables, and probably in the dreams of every chef. In Greece, "extra olives" is a redundant phrase – it's always extra olives.

GREENLAND
Denmark

Far North
population: 56,583
Size (sq miles): 836,330
Size (sq km):   2,166,086

Where Icebergs Are Bigger Than Buildings: In Greenland, icebergs aren't just floating ice cubes; they're like nature's skyscrapers. Some are so massive they have their own ecosystems. It's like Mother Nature decided to try her hand at ice sculpture, and she went big. Cruising among these icy giants, you feel like a tiny character in a frozen storybook.

Midnight Sun and Polar Nights: Depending on the time of year, Greenland either barely sleeps or barely wakes up. During summer, the sun doesn't set for weeks in the northern parts, leading to the famous midnight sun. It's perfect for night owls - who needs sleep when you've got 24-hour daylight? Conversely, winter brings the polar night - when the sun doesn't rise at all, making every hour perfect for hot cocoa.

Dog Sledding: The Greenlandic Way to Travel: Forget cars; in Greenland, dog sledding is a traditional way to get around. It's like a taxi service, but more furry and with more barking. These sled dogs are not just pets; they're hardworking, four-legged locals who know how to navigate the icy terrain better than any GPS could. Riding a dog sled is like stepping back in time, only with more fur and less Wi-Fi.

GRENADA

Carribbean
population: 124,610
Size (sq miles): 134.6
Size (sq km): 348.5

Nutmeg in the Air: Grenada is known as the "Isle of Spice," especially famous for nutmeg. Walking through the markets, it's like you've entered a giant spice cabinet. They produce so much nutmeg here; you might start to wonder if there's a secret nutmeg party you're not invited to. Remember, in Grenada, a pinch of nutmeg goes a long way – like into every dish!

The Underwater Sculpture Park: Grenada boasts the world's first underwater sculpture park. It's like an art gallery, but you'll need a snorkel instead of a ticket. These sculptures aren't just cool to look at; they're also part of a reef regeneration project. It's where art meets conservation, and fish are the regular visitors.

Calypso Music: The Soundtrack of the Island: In Grenada, calypso music is not just a genre; it's a way of life. The island pulses with rhythms and lyrics that tell stories, celebrate life, and get everyone dancing. It's like the island has its own soundtrack, and everyone's living in a musical. If you're in Grenada and your feet aren't tapping, you're probably asleep!

GUADELOUPE
France

Carribbean
population: 378,561
Size (sq miles): 629
Size (sq km): 1,628

A Butterfly-Shaped Island: Guadeloupe is unique because it's shaped like a butterfly – Grande-Terre and Basse-Terre are its wings. It's like Mother Nature decided to get creative with geography. This means you can tell friends you're vacationing on the left or right wing of a butterfly. And who knows, maybe you'll get butterfly kisses from the gentle sea breeze!

Rum: The Spirit of the Island: In Guadeloupe, rum isn't just a drink; it's a cultural icon. They love their rum so much, there are more distilleries than towns. Tasting rum here is like going on a flavorful adventure, where each sip tells a story of the island's history and heritage. Just remember, too much rum and you might start seeing double...butterflies.

Gwo Ka: Drum Beats and Street Dancing: Gwo Ka is not just music; it's an expression of Guadeloupe's soul. It combines African drum rhythms with dance and song. Participating in a Gwo Ka is like joining a spontaneous street party. The rhythm is infectious – you might find your body moving before your brain even agrees. It's like the island has its own heartbeat, and it's set to the rhythm of the drums.

GUAM
United States

Oceania
population: 168,801
Size (sq miles): 210
Size (sq km): 540

First to Greet the Sun in the US: Guam is where America's day begins, thanks to its location in the western Pacific. It's like the island is the early bird of the US, catching the sunrise while the rest of the country is still hitting snooze. Living in Guam means you're literally living in the future compared to your friends on the mainland.

Latte Stones - Not Your Average Coffee Order: In Guam, 'latte' doesn't just refer to a coffee drink. Latte Stones are ancient pillars used by the indigenous Chamorro people. These aren't just any old rocks; they're like the Stonehenge of the Pacific, only less crowded and with more tropical vibes. You can't drink them, but they're still pretty impressive.

Fiesta Time: Food, Family, and Fun: In Guam, fiestas are a big deal. They're like the ultimate block party, but with better food and everyone's invited. These gatherings are a fusion of Chamorro traditions, Spanish influences, and American flair. Attending a fiesta in Guam is like entering a marathon of eating, laughing, and more eating. Just remember, in Guam, "I'm full" is considered a temporary condition.

GUATEMALA

Central America
population: 17,980,803
Size (sq miles): 42,042
Size (sq km):   108,889

Tikal: Where the Mayans Left Their Mark: Guatemala is home to Tikal, one of the largest ancient Mayan cities. These ruins aren't just a bunch of old stones; they're like the skyscrapers of the past, minus the elevators and with more toucans. Exploring Tikal is like walking into a 'Jungle Book' story, only with temples and pyramids instead of singing bears.

Lake Atitlán: A Lake Guarded by Volcanoes: Lake Atitlán is not your average lake. It's flanked by three majestic volcanoes, making it look like a postcard come to life. It's as if the lake called dibs on the best natural backdrop. Whether you're kayaking or just chilling lakeside, the view is like a triple-threat of nature's beauty.

A Riot of Color in Every Thread: Guatemalan textiles are a kaleidoscope of colors. These aren't just fabrics; they're stories woven by hand, each pattern telling a tale of tradition and culture. Wearing these textiles is like donning a piece of history – but way more fashionable and less dusty than actual history. And in Guatemala, "clashing colors" isn't a fashion faux pas; it's a fashion statement.

GUERNSEY
United Kingdom

Western Europe
population: 63,950
Size (sq miles): 24
Size (sq km): 62

The Island That Inspired a Bestseller: Guernsey is not just another pretty island – it inspired the novel "The Guernsey Literary and Potato Peel Pie Society." It's like the island auditioned for a book role and got the part. Strolling through Guernsey's picturesque lanes and historic harbors, you can almost hear the whispers of stories waiting to be told, or at least turned into a delicious potato peel pie.

Guernsey Cows: The Dairy Queens: Guernsey cows are more than just regular cows; they're like the supermodels of the bovine world. Famous for their rich, creamy milk, they're the reason why the island's butter and cream are so deliciously famous. In Guernsey, "milk run" might involve meeting a local celebrity on four legs.

A Stone's Throw from Everywhere: Guernsey's location near France and the UK makes it a cultural crossroads. The island is the neighborhood hangout for both countries. Whether you fancy a French croissant or a British scone, in Guernsey, you're just a stone's throw away from a continental culinary adventure. Plus, with a mix of French street names and English pubs, it's like the island couldn't quite decide on its favorite neighbor.

GUINEA-BISSAU

West Africa
population: 2,078,820
Size (sq miles): 13,948
Size (sq km):   36,125

Archipelago Adventures: Guinea-Bissau boasts the Bijagós Archipelago, a group of islands so pristine and untouched, it seems they missed the memo on modernization. It's like nature's own secret garden, but with more fish and fewer gates. Visiting these islands is like stepping into a real-life screensaver – just without the computer.

The Land Where Cashews Reign Supreme: In Guinea-Bissau, cashew nuts aren't just a snack; they're a way of life. The country is one of the world's top cashew producers. Here, 'going nuts' takes on a whole new meaning, especially during harvest season. It's like every tree decided to join the cashew craze – and the locals are definitely not complaining.

Gumbe: The Rhythm of the Land: If Guinea-Bissau had a soundtrack, it would be set to the rhythm of Gumbe. This musical genre, with its infectious beats and spirited dance moves, is the heart of the country's cultural scene. Engaging in a Gumbe session is like jumping into a whirlpool of drums and joy – it's impossible not to get swept up in the rhythm. In Guinea-Bissau, 'losing the beat' means you're probably dancing to your own (equally fun) drummer.

GUINEA

West Africa
population: 14,190,612
Size (sq miles): 94,926
Size (sq km): 245,857

Waterfalls That Put Your Shower to Shame: In Guinea, they take their waterfalls seriously. The country is home to the stunning Chutes de la Tinkisso and many others, where the water doesn't just fall; it performs. It's like nature's version of Broadway, but with more splashing and less singing. Visiting these waterfalls is like stepping into a natural shower, only more epic and with fewer shampoo bottles.

Markets Bursting with Life and Color: The markets in Guinea are like a party where everyone's invited, and the dress code is 'colorful.' From Conakry's bustling markets to smaller village bazaars, each one is a kaleidoscope of fabrics, foods, and crafts. Shopping here isn't just a transaction; it's an adventure in haggling, laughing, and making new friends – sometimes all at once.

The Kora: Not Your Average Harp: In Guinea, the kora, a 21-stringed instrument, reigns supreme. It's like a harp and a lute had a beautiful musical baby. The sound of the kora is so enchanting, it's like being serenaded by the history and spirit of West Africa. Listening to a kora player is like attending a concert that's part storytelling, part history lesson, and all melody.

GUYANA

South America
population: 795,408
Size (sq miles): 83,000
Size (sq km):   215,000

Kaieteur Falls: Where Water Takes a Mighty Leap: In Guyana, Kaieteur Falls isn't just a trickle of water; it's a colossal cascade four times higher than Niagara Falls. It's as if the river decides to take a dramatic plunge, showing off its power and beauty. Visiting Kaieteur is like witnessing nature's own version of a blockbuster action movie, only wetter.

A Nation Crazy for Cricket: Guyana's love for cricket is as vast as its rainforests. It's not just a sport; it's a cultural event where every hit and run is discussed with the same enthusiasm as a presidential election. Joining a cricket match in Guyana is like stepping into a festival of cheers, groans, and spirited debates. It's the island's unofficial party, and everyone's invited.

A Biodiversity Hotspot Like No Other: Guyana is a paradise for nature enthusiasts, boasting one of the most pristine rainforests in South America. It's home to exotic wildlife, from jaguars to giant otters. Exploring Guyana's natural wonders is like stepping onto the set of a wildlife documentary, except the birds, animals, and trees are the real celebrities here. Remember, in Guyana, the star of the show is always Mother Nature.

HAITI

Carribbean
population: 11,470,261
Size (sq miles): 10,710
Size (sq km): 27,750

The Citadel: A Fortress on a Hill: Haiti is home to the Citadelle Laferrière, a massive stone fortress perched atop a mountain. Built after independence from France, it's like Haiti's version of the Great Wall – only steeper and with more stories to tell. The trek to the Citadel is a workout, but the views and history lesson at the top are worth every panting breath.

Art Everywhere You Look: In Haiti, art isn't confined to galleries; it's a part of everyday life. Vibrant murals adorn the streets, and hand-painted 'tap-taps' (local buses) turn daily commutes into moving art shows. Haitian art is a burst of color, emotion, and story – it's like the country wears its heart on its canvas.

The Resilience and Rhythms of the People: Haitians are known for their resilience and strength, having overcome great challenges. This resilience is mirrored in their rich cultural heritage, especially in music and dance. Rara and Kompa music, with their infectious beats, tell stories of struggle, joy, and everyday life. Dancing in Haiti is not just for fun; it's a way of expression, a celebration of life's ups and downs. In Haiti, when the music starts, everyone – young and old – is part of the dance floor.

HONDURAS

Central America
population: 9,571,352
Size (sq miles): 43,433
Size (sq km): 112,492

Copán Ruins: Where the Mayans Left Their Mark: In Honduras, the Copán Ruins are a testament to the ancient Mayan civilization. It's like walking into a history book, except the pictures are real stone carvings and the chapters are written in hieroglyphics. Exploring Copán is like being an archaeologist, but without the dust and with more selfie opportunities.

The Bird of a Thousand Colors: The Scarlet Macaw: Honduras is home to the vibrant scarlet macaw, a bird so colorful, it looks like it flew through a rainbow. These birds aren't just pretty; they're like the pop stars of the animal kingdom, flaunting their colors and squawking catchy tunes. In Honduras, birdwatching is more like a fashion show with wings.

Diving into the Mesoamerican Reef: Off the coast of Honduras lies the Mesoamerican Barrier Reef, the second-largest coral reef in the world. Diving here is like entering an underwater carnival, with colorful corals, fish, and maybe the occasional curious turtle. It's a world where 'traffic' means schools of fish, and the only 'road rage' is between competing clownfish.

HONG KONG
China

Eastern Asia
population: 7,498,100
Size (sq miles): 1,063.70
Size (sq km): 2,754.97

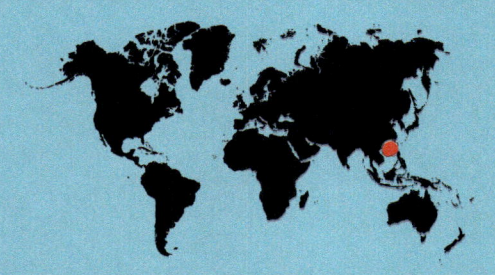

A Forest of Skyscrapers: Hong Kong might hold the record for the most skyscrapers in the world (sorry NYC). It's like the buildings are in a constant competition to touch the sky. The city's skyline is a concrete jungle gym, where each skyscraper is trying to outdo its neighbor. At night, they light up like a giant's Christmas tree, only more stylish and with fewer pine needles.

Dim Sum: A Culinary Adventure in Bite-Sized Portions: In Hong Kong, dim sum is not just a meal; it's a weekend ritual. These bite-sized delights come in an endless variety, from shrimp dumplings to BBQ pork buns. Eating dim sum is like playing a tasty game of edible roulette – you never know what you'll pick next, but it's always a delicious surprise.

Dragon Dances: When Mythical Creatures Take to the Streets: The dragon dance is a vital part of many celebrations, especially Chinese New Year. These aren't your average dragons; they're colorful, energetic, and often require multiple people to bring them to life. Watching a dragon dance in Hong Kong is like seeing a mythical creature joyously galloping down the street, and everyone's invited to join the party. Just remember, it's considered bad luck to step on a dragon's tail, even if it's made of silk.

HUNGARY

Eastern Europe
population: 9,597,085
Size (sq miles): 35,920
Size (sq km):   93,030

Soak in a City of Spas: Budapest, Hungary's capital, is sometimes called the "City of Spas." With more thermal and medicinal water springs than any other capital in the world, it's like the city decided to become one giant wellness retreat. Here, taking a bath isn't just about getting clean; it's a social event, a historical journey, and sometimes, a game of chess in the water.

Paprika: The Spice of Hungarian Life: In Hungary, paprika isn't just a spice; it's practically a national symbol. This red powder appears in almost every traditional dish, from goulash to chicken paprikash. It's like Hungarians decided that food is better when it's a little bit red and a lot spicy. In Hungary, "a pinch of paprika" is a bit of an understatement.

Hungarian: Not Your Average Language: The Hungarian language is known for being notoriously difficult to learn, with complex grammar and a melody all its own. It's like the language took a regular grammar book and said, "No, thanks, I'll dance to my own tune." Learning to say "hello" (szia) might make you feel like a linguistic gymnast, but the smiles you'll receive in return are totally worth the workout.

ICELAND

Northern Europe
population: 399,189
Size (sq miles): 39,817
Size (sq km): 103,125

Volcanoes and Glaciers – A Chilly and Hot Mix: Iceland is famously known as the land of fire and ice. It's like nature couldn't decide between a winter wonderland and a volcanic playground, so it chose both. Here, you can visit a glacier and a volcano in the same day – just make sure to pack both a winter jacket and heat-resistant boots.

Elves: Iceland's Hidden Residents: Many Icelanders believe in elves, or 'Huldufólk', hidden people living in rocks. It's like a fairy tale, but in real life. Construction projects often take these unseen residents into account, just in case. It's always good to stay on the friendly side of your elf neighbors, especially when they're known for their mischief!

Golf at Midnight, Anyone?: Thanks to the midnight sun during summer, you can literally play golf at midnight in Iceland. It's perfect for those who think a normal round of golf isn't quite adventurous enough. Imagine teeing off under a sky that refuses to get dark; it's like nature's own nightlight, ensuring you never lose your golf ball again (well, maybe).

INDIA

South Asia
population: 1,428,627,663
Size (sq miles): 1,269,219
Size (sq km):   3,287,263

A Tower of Babel in One Country: In India, saying "hello" can sound different every few miles. With over 22 major languages and hundreds of dialects, it's like the country decided to have a language buffet. You might start the day with a 'Namaste,' have a 'Vanakkam' for lunch, and end with a 'Shubha ratri,' all without leaving the country.

The Taj Mahal: The Taj Mahal isn't just another beautiful monument. It's a grand declaration of love, built by an emperor in memory of his wife. It's like he said, "Flowers are nice, but have you tried a marble tomb?" Visiting the Taj Mahal is a must – it's like stepping into a postcard, only better because you can actually walk around in it.

Cricket: A Religion Disguised as a Sport: In India, cricket is not just a game; it's a religion, and Sachin Tendulkar is a demigod. The country stops for major cricket matches. It's like an unofficial national holiday, complete with rituals, prayers, and nail-biting suspense. And if you ever want to strike up a conversation in India, just ask about cricket – you'll make friends for life.

INDONESIA

Southeast Asia
population: 279,118,866
Size (sq miles): 735,358
Size (sq km): 1,904,569

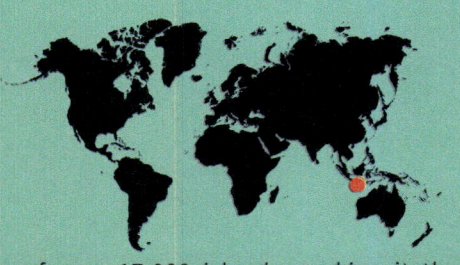

So Many Islands: Indonesia is made up of over 17,000 islands, making it the world's largest archipelago. It's like Indonesia won a geography jackpot and decided to keep every island it got. From the bustling streets of Java to the tranquil beaches of Bali, each island offers a new adventure. You could spend a lifetime island-hopping here and still have more to see – pack accordingly!

Volcanoes as Far as the Eye Can See: Indonesia sits on the Pacific Ring of Fire, so volcanoes are a big part of the landscape. With over 130 active volcanoes, it's like the country is playing a game of volcanic chess with nature. Hiking these majestic mountains offers breathtaking views and a little thrill – because you're never quite sure when they might say 'hello.'

Wayang Kulit: The Shadow Puppet Show: Wayang kulit, the traditional Indonesian shadow puppetry, is a unique blend of art and storytelling. It's like watching ancient myths and legends come to life, but in silhouette. A single performance can last all night – it's the original Netflix binge-watching, only with more shadows and less screen time.

IRAN

Middle East
population: 87,590,873
Size (sq miles): 636,372
Size (sq km):   1,648,195

Persepolis: The Echoes of Ancient Glory: In Iran, the ruins of Persepolis stand as a testament to the ancient Persian Empire. Walking through its grand columns and majestic staircases is like time traveling to 500 B.C., but without the hassle of figuring out a time machine. It's like visiting a real-life version of a history book, except more impressive and with fewer quizzes.

Poetry Runs in the Veins: Iranians have poetry in their soul. Here, poets like Hafez and Rumi aren't just read; they're celebrated. It's like poetry is the national language, and everyone is fluent in it. Don't be surprised if a casual conversation turns into a poetic exchange – it's just the Iranian way.

Persian Carpets: More Than Just Floor Coverings: In Iran, Persian carpets are a big deal. Each carpet is not just a decor item; it's a work of art, often taking years to complete. Walking into an Iranian home is like stepping onto a canvas of intricate designs and vibrant colors. And remember, in Iran, spilling something on a Persian carpet is more than an accident; it's a cultural faux pas.

IRAQ

Middle East
population: 43,324,000
Size (sq miles): 169,235
Size (sq km): 438,317

Cradle of Civilization: Where History Began: Iraq is often called the "Cradle of Civilization," as it was home to ancient Mesopotamia. This is where some of the world's earliest cities, like Babylon and Ur, flourished. Walking through Iraq is like wandering through the pages of history, except the ruins are real, and there are no pop-up ads.

Tigris and Euphrates: Rivers of Legends: The Tigris and Euphrates, two of the most famous rivers in history, flow through Iraq. They're not just bodies of water; they're like the main characters in the story of civilization. If these rivers could talk, they'd probably never stop, given how much they've seen. Fishing or just strolling along their banks is like a meet-and-greet with ancient legends.

A Nation of Unmatched Hospitality: Despite its tumultuous history, Iraqis are known for their incredible hospitality. It's like the whole country decided to be the best host in the world. In Iraq, a guest is treated like royalty, often with more food than they can possibly eat – refusing a second helping might require diplomatic skills! Remember, in Iraq, "Make yourself at home" isn't just a saying; it's a command.

IRELAND

Western Europe
population: 5,281,600
Size (sq miles): 27,133
Size (sq km):   70,273

A Castle Around Every Corner: In Ireland, it seems there's a castle for every day of the year, and then some. From the dramatic ruins of Dunluce Castle to the stately elegance of Dublin Castle, these stone fortresses are like Ireland's version of a home improvement show – medieval edition. Exploring these castles is like stepping back in time, except with fewer knights and more tourists.

The Gift of the Gab at Blarney Stone: According to legend, kissing the Blarney Stone at Blarney Castle bestows the gift of eloquence, or as the Irish call it, "the gift of the gab." It's an acrobatic feat that involves bending backward and smooching a stone - like a reverse trust fall with a historical twist. Just remember, eloquence might be just a kiss away, but so is a weird backache.

Craic: In Ireland, 'craic' (pronounced like 'crack') is all about having a good time. It's the art of enjoying life, with a bit of humor and a lot of good conversation. Going to a pub in Ireland isn't just about the drink; it's about the craic. It's where stories are spun, laughs are had, and friends are made. In Ireland, if you're not having the craic, you're not doing it right!

ISLE OF MAN
United Kingdom

Western Europe
population: 84,069
Size (sq miles): 222
Size (sq km): 574

Manx Cats: The Unique Tailless Felines: The Isle of Man is famous for its native breed of cat, the Manx, known for its distinctive lack of a tail. It's like these cats decided tails were last season and opted for a more streamlined look. These unique felines are as much a part of the island as the rolling hills and rugged coastlines.

The TT Race: Not Your Average Bike Ride: The Isle of Man TT (Tourist Trophy) Race is one of the most dangerous and thrilling motorcycle races in the world. It's like the island turns into a high-speed racetrack, where the only speed bumps are the occasional sheep crossing. Watching the TT races is like seeing motorbikes transformed into lightning bolts – just with more noise and adrenaline.

A Land Believing in Fairies: The Isle of Man is steeped in folklore, including a firm belief in fairies. Locals often greet the 'Little People' when crossing the Fairy Bridge, to avoid bad luck. It's like the island has its own magical guardians, and it's just polite to say hello. So, remember, a quick nod to the fairies might just make your stay a little more magical.

ISRAEL

Middle East
population: 9,849,920
Size (sq miles): 8,470
Size (sq km): 21,937

A Melting Pot of Ancient and Modern: In Israel, ancient history rubs shoulders with modern life. You can walk through millennia-old sites like the Western Wall in Jerusalem, then catch a high-tech startup pitch in Tel Aviv. It's like the country is on a first-name basis with both King David and Mark Zuckerberg.

Tel Aviv's Beach: The Unofficial Office: In Tel Aviv, the beach is more than just a place to relax; it's a way of life. With golden sands and Mediterranean blues, it's like the city decided to have a board meeting and a beach party at the same time. You'll see people in suits, bikinis, and sometimes a combination of both.

Hebrew: The Lazarus of Languages: Hebrew is one of the greatest comeback stories in language history. Once out of everyday use, it was revived and modernized, transforming from ancient scripts to daily chats. It's like Hebrew was a language superhero that came out of retirement. Now, it's spoken by millions, proving that you can teach an old language new words.

ITALY

Southern Europe
population: 58,853,482
Size (sq miles): 116,350
Size (sq km):   301,340

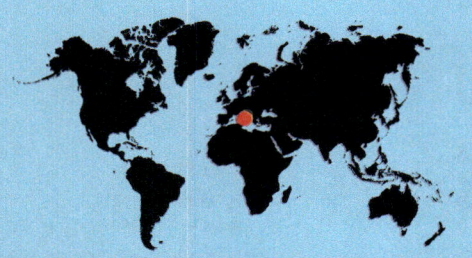

The Leaning Tower of Pisa: Italy's Tipsy Tower: The Leaning Tower of Pisa is famous worldwide for doing what most buildings try not to do – lean. It's like the tower tried to do a bit of yoga and got stuck in the pose. Tourists love pretending to hold it up or push it down, because who doesn't like a bit of interactive architecture?

Pasta: An Edible Art Form: In Italy, pasta isn't just food; it's a culinary art. There are over 300 shapes of pasta, and each region has its favorite. It's like each type of pasta is a different brush stroke in Italy's culinary masterpiece. From al dente spaghetti to stuffed ravioli, every meal is a 'mamma mia' moment.

Expressive Hand Gestures: A Language of Their Own: Italians are known for their expressive hand gestures. It's like they have an entire conversation with their hands. In Italy, you don't just listen with your ears; you watch the hands, too. It's a place where "talk to the hand" has a whole different meaning – it's part of the dialogue!

JAMAICA

Carribbean
population: 2,734,092
Size (sq miles): 4,244
Size (sq km):   10,991

The Home of Reggae and Bob Marley: Jamaica is the birthplace of reggae music, and the legendary Bob Marley is its most famous son. It's like the whole island moves to a reggae rhythm - even the trees seem to sway more rhythmically here. Visiting the Bob Marley Museum in Kingston is like stepping into the heart of reggae, only with fewer dreadlocks and more souvenirs.

Sprinting Superstars: Jamaica is renowned for producing some of the world's fastest sprinters, like Usain Bolt. It's as if there's something in the water (or the jerk chicken) that makes people run like the wind. In Jamaica, 'taking it slow' applies to everything but sprinting.

Jerk Spice: Not Just a Seasoning, but a Way of Life: Jerk spice is a big deal in Jamaica. It's a magical blend of spices that can transform chicken, pork, or even vegetables into a mouth-watering meal. Eating jerk in Jamaica is like embarking on a spicy, smoky flavor adventure - one that might require a cold drink on standby. In Jamaica, 'jerk' is a good thing, at least when it comes to food.

JAPAN

Eastern Asia
population: 125,416,877
Size (sq miles): 145,937
Size (sq km):   377,975

Island Hopping Adventure: Picture a country made up of more than 6,800 islands. That's Japan! It's like a giant puzzle, with islands scattered in the ocean. The four main islands are Honshu, Hokkaido, Kyushu, and Shikoku. Imagine one day skiing down snowy slopes and the next day playing on sunny beaches – all in the same country!

Amazing Monuments: In Japan, you can find a temple guarded by deer! That's right, in Nara, the deer roam freely around the Todai-ji Temple, which has a huge Buddha statue. They're super friendly and might even pose for a selfie with you. And in Tokyo, there's a giant tower painted in bright orange and white called the Tokyo Tower. It's like a colorful version of the Eiffel Tower, but it's totally Japanese style!

Festivals Full of Fun: Japan loves festivals, and one of the most exciting is the Tanabata Festival. People write their wishes on colorful pieces of paper and hang them on bamboo trees, hoping the stars will make their wishes come true. The streets get filled with bright decorations and everyone has a blast.

JERSEY
United Kingdom

Western Europe
population: 103,267
Size (sq miles): 46.2
Size (sq km): 119.6

Geography Giggles: Jersey might be small, but it's got a superpower: it changes size! Not really, but thanks to the tide, Jersey can almost double in size twice a day. When the tide goes out, new beaches and pathways appear like magic. It's like playing hide and seek with the sea!

Monumental Mischief: In Jersey, even the castles have secrets. Mont Orgueil Castle has hidden rooms and secret passageways that were used to protect it from invaders. Legend says there might still be hidden treasures lurking around. So, if you visit, keep your eyes peeled – you might just stumble upon a centuries-old secret!

Crazy Customs: Ever seen a parade of flowers? In Jersey, they have the Battle of Flowers, a festival where floats covered in flowers parade through the streets. It started over 100 years ago as a royal celebration, and now it's like a flower-powered party on wheels. The best part? The day after the parade, there's a moonlight parade where all the floats light up, turning the night into a twinkling flower wonderland.

JORDAN

Middle East
population: 11,484,805
Size (sq miles): 34,495
Size (sq km):   89,342

Sandy Surprises: Think deserts are just endless sand? Jordan's Wadi Rum will prove you wrong! It's not just any desert; it's a Mars lookalike with red sands and towering cliffs. Hollywood loves it so much, it's been a movie star more times than some actors. So, if you visit, you might just be walking on a real-life movie set!

Petra: The Hide-and-Seek City: Jordan is home to Petra, an ancient city carved into pink cliffs. It's like the city decided to play hide and seek and never stopped! For centuries, it was hidden from the world until a Swiss explorer rediscovered it in 1812. Now, it's no secret that this wonder is a must-see, especially when it lights up at night with thousands of candles. Talk about a grand entrance!

Floating Fun: The Dead Sea, bordering Jordan with Israel, is so salty you can float without trying. It's like nature's own inflatable pool, but saltier! Here, swimming means lounging on the water's surface, and don't forget to slather on some of the famous Dead Sea mud – it's like a free spa treatment!

KAZAKHSTAN

Central Asia
population: 20,000,000
Size (sq miles): 1,052,100
Size (sq km):   2,724,900

Space and Steppe: Kazakhstan is out-of-this-world – literally! The Baikonur Cosmodrome here is the world's first and largest space launch facility. It's like a space taxi stand, but for astronauts! Back on Earth, the vast steppes of Kazakhstan stretch far and wide, where you can travel for hours without seeing a single soul – perfect for when you need a break from your annoying siblings.

Singing Sand Dunes: In the Altyn-Emel National Park, there are sand dunes that sing! Well, they don't exactly belt out pop hits, but when the wind blows, these dunes hum mysteriously. It's like the desert's own natural soundtrack. Maybe the sands are just trying to start their own band?

Apple of Your Eye: Ever wonder where apples came from? Thank Kazakhstan! The city of Almaty, which means 'Father of Apples', is home to the ancestor of all modern apples. So, every time you munch on an apple, remember, it's got some Kazakh roots. Who knew apples could have such a well-traveled family tree?

KENYA

East Africa
population: 51,526,000
Size (sq miles): 224,081
Size (sq km):   580,367

The Safari Capital of the World: Kenya is like nature's theme park, famous for its safaris in the Maasai Mara. Here, you can see the 'Big Five' - lion, leopard, rhinoceros, elephant, and buffalo – like the most exciting roll call ever. It's a place where zebras and giraffes are the locals, and tourists are the ones in cages (well, safari vehicles).

Home of Champions - Long-Distance Running Stars: In Kenya, running is not just a sport; it's a way of life, especially in the Rift Valley. Here, running a marathon is less of a 'bucket list' item and more of a daily commute. Kenyan runners are so fast; they could probably give the cheetahs a run for their money.

The Maasai's Adumu: Not Just a Dance, But a Show of Strength: The Maasai's traditional jumping dance, the Adumu, is a sight to behold. It's like a high-stakes game of 'The Floor Is Lava,' but where the goal is to touch the sky. Watching the Maasai warriors jump, you might start wondering if they have springs in their legs. And if you try joining in, you'll quickly realize it's harder than it looks – it's like the Maasai version of a gym workout.

KIRIBATI

Oceania
population: 121,388
Size (sq miles): 313.20
Size (sq km):   811.19

Time Travelers: Did you know Kiribati is the first country to see the sunrise each day? It's like they live in the future! The International Date Line was specially bent just to keep all of Kiribati on the same day. So, if you're in Kiribati on New Year's Eve, you'll be among the first in the world to welcome the New Year. Party in the future, anyone?

The Disappearing Act: Kiribati is made up of 33 atolls and islands, but here's the catch – some are so flat and low-lying that during high tide, some of them almost disappear! It's like playing peek-a-boo with islands. Imagine telling your friends, "Sorry, I can't come over, my island is hiding!"

Dancing with Frigatebirds: In Kiribati culture, the frigatebird is a big deal. There's even a traditional dance mimicking its movements. Picture this: dancers gracefully flapping their arms, imitating the bird's flight. It's like a feathery flash mob! This dance is a unique way to honor nature, show off some smooth moves, and maybe even get a laugh.

KOSOVO

Southeast Europe
population: 1,761,985
Size (sq miles): 4,203
Size (sq km):   10,887

Coffee Culture Kings: In Kosovo, coffee isn't just a drink; it's a national pastime! The traditional coffee, similar to Turkish coffee, is super strong and served in tiny cups. It's like a magical potion to wake you up. People spend hours chatting over coffee, so if you're invited for a coffee in Kosovo, clear your schedule – it's going to be a long and chatty adventure!

Bear Sanctuary Superstars: Kosovo is home to the Four Paws Bear Sanctuary, where rescued bears live like celebrities. These bears had a rough start in life, but now they're living the dream with spacious habitats and plenty of pampering. Visitors can watch these furry VIPs lounge, play, and strut their stuff. It's like a spa retreat, but for bears!

A Young Heart: Kosovo is Europe's youngest country in terms of independence and also in terms of its population. With so many young people around, the vibe is energetic and vibrant. It's like the whole country is in the midst of its youthful prime – full of life, creativity, and a dash of rebellious spirit. Kosovo's youthful energy makes it a dynamic and lively place to explore.

KUWAIT

Middle East
population: 4,294,621
Size (sq miles): 6,880
Size (sq km): 17,818

Towers with a Twist: Kuwait is famous for its Kuwait Towers, which look like they came straight out of a sci-fi movie! These aren't your regular towers; they're decorated with blue-green sequins, making them sparkle in the sun. It's like the towers got dressed up for a glamorous party and never changed back!

The Singing Sands: In the deserts of Kuwait, the sands don't just sit there; they sing! When the wind blows just right, the sands can make a humming noise. It's as if the desert is trying to start its own choir. Maybe the sands are just practicing for Kuwait's next big talent show?

Diwaniya – Where Chats Happen: In Kuwaiti culture, there's a tradition called Diwaniya – a gathering where men come together to discuss everything from politics to sports. Think of it as a social club, but in someone's living room with lots of tea and snacks. It's like the original social network, but with better refreshments and no internet trolls!

KYRGYZSTAN

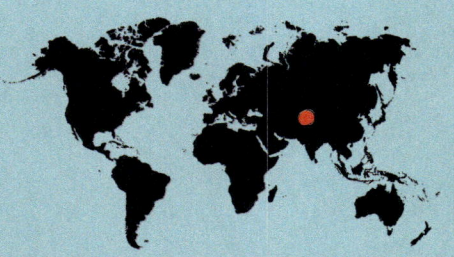

Central Asia
population: 7,037,590
Size (sq miles): 77,202
Size (sq km): 199,951

Lake Issyk-Kul: The Beach in the Mountains: In Kyrgyzstan, you can sunbathe at a beach surrounded by snowy peaks! Lake Issyk-Kul, the world's second-largest mountain lake, never freezes – even in the chilliest winters. It's like having a giant, natural hot tub in the middle of a snowy landscape. Who needs the sea when you have a warm lake in the mountains?

Burana Tower: Leaning with Style: The Burana Tower in Kyrgyzstan is a bit like the Leaning Tower of Pisa's less famous cousin. This ancient tower is all that's left of a city from the 9th century and has its own quirky tilt. It's as if it's trying to do a little dance or maybe just peering over at the tourists.

Nomadic Nosh: Beshbarmak: In Kyrgyzstan, the national dish Beshbarmak takes 'meat and potatoes' to a whole new level. It's a hearty mix of noodles, onions, and horse meat (yes, horse!). Beshbarmak means 'five fingers' because it's traditionally eaten with your hands. It's like the ultimate finger food, but don't worry, napkins are allowed!

LAOS

Southeast Asia
population: 7,749,595
Size (sq miles): 91,400
Size (sq km): 236,800

The Elephant Parade: In Laos, elephants are not just animals; they're like the big, friendly giants of the nation. There's even an annual Elephant Festival where these majestic creatures are celebrated with parades and shows. It's like a giant party, but the guests of honor weigh over 3,000 pounds and love to munch on bananas!

Kuang Si Falls: The Swimming Pool of Nature: Imagine a waterfall that looks like it's straight out of a fantasy movie. That's Kuang Si Falls in Laos. With its turquoise blue waters and multiple levels, it's like nature's own waterpark. The best part? You can actually swim in these natural pools. Who needs chlorine when you've got Mother Nature's own recipe for fun?

Sticky Rice Galore: In Laos, sticky rice is not just a side dish; it's a way of life. Eaten with almost every meal, it's like the Laotian version of bread or potatoes. The fun part? You eat it with your hands, rolling it into little balls. It's like playdough that you can eat, only much tastier and less salty!

LATVIA

Eastern Europe · Baltic States
population: 1,842,226
Size (sq miles): 24,938
Size (sq km): 64,589

A Nation in Tune: Latvia might just be the world's most musical country. Every five years, they host the Latvian Song and Dance Festival, where literally thousands of singers and dancers come together. Imagine your whole country singing in harmony – it's like Latvia is one giant choir! And with more than a million folk songs, they probably have a song for everything, even for brushing your teeth.

Riga's House of Cats: In the capital city of Riga, there's a building famous for its rooftop cats. Yes, cats! These feline statues are perched on the turrets, looking like they're about to pounce. Legend has it, they were put there by a disgruntled merchant to face his rivals. It's like the ultimate cat stare-down, but in statue form.

Forest Fanatics: Latvians love their forests so much, they cover almost half the country! It's like living in a giant green wonderland. They even celebrate "Jāņi" by going into the woods, wearing wreaths made of flowers and leaves. Imagine having a party with trees as your party guests – talk about being one with nature!

LEBANON

Middle East
population: 5,296,814
Size (sq miles): 4,036
Size (sq km): 10,452

Beirut: The Phoenix City: Beirut, Lebanon's capital, is like the comeback kid of cities. It has been rebuilt seven times after various disasters. It's like the city looks at destruction and says, "Is that all you've got?" Today, though still going through hard times, it's a bustling, vibrant city, where history meets modernity in a lively dance of culture and cuisine.

Cedars of God: In Lebanon, trees get VIP treatment, especially the famous Cedars of God. These ancient trees are so important they're even on the country's flag! Imagine a tree so cool, it gets to be a national symbol. Visiting these cedars is like stepping into a living history book, except with more leaves and fewer pages.

Hummus: More Than Just a Dip: In Lebanon, hummus isn't just a snack; it's a source of national pride. This creamy, chickpea delight is taken very seriously. Lebanese hummus is like the gold standard – smooth, rich, and often a topic of friendly debate: "Who makes the best hummus?" It's not just food; it's an art form, a tradition, and maybe even a competitive sport!

LESOTHO

Southern Africa
population: 2,210,646
Size (sq miles): 11,720
Size (sq km): 30,355

A Country on Stilts: Lesotho is known as the 'Kingdom in the Sky' because it's the only country in the world that's entirely above 1,000 meters! It's like living on a giant natural skyscraper. Even their lowest point is higher than the tallest buildings in many countries. Talk about living the high life!

Pony Trekking Adventures: In Lesotho, the best way to travel is on a Basotho pony. These sturdy little horses are the local taxis. They're like the 4x4s of the horse world, perfect for navigating the mountainous terrain. So, when in Lesotho, forget cars, get yourself a pony!

The Fashion of Blankets: In Lesotho, blankets aren't just for keeping warm; they're a fashion statement. The Basotho people wear their colorful blankets with pride, each design telling a different story. It's like their version of a tailored suit, but cozier and with more stories to tell. You haven't truly experienced Lesotho until you've wrapped yourself in a Basotho blanket!

LIBERIA

West Africa
population: 5,506,280
Size (sq miles): 43,000
Size (sq km): 111,370

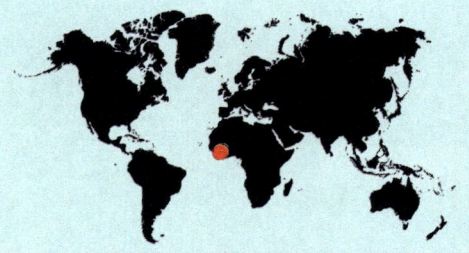

A Capital with a Tale: Monrovia, the capital of Liberia, is the only capital in the world (outside the US) named after a U.S. President, James Monroe. People of Liberia liked him so much, they named their city after him! It's one of the many signs of the unique historical ties Liberia shares with the United States. Another hint: look at the flag...

Rainforests Galore: Liberia is like the VIP lounge for rainforests. It's home to some of West Africa's last remaining rainforests, where trees throw shade like it's going out of style. These forests aren't just pretty; they're like nature's own amusement parks, full of exotic animals and plants you won't find at your local zoo.

The Land of Long Names: In Liberia, people love giving their children long and unique names. Some names are so long, they're like mini-stories! Imagine having a name that takes up the whole attendance sheet in school. It's like each person is walking around with their own personal motto or a mini-biography!

LIBYA

North Africa
population: 7,252,573
Size (sq miles): 679,363
Size (sq km): 1,759,541

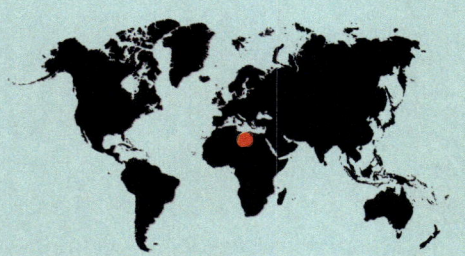

Sahara's Ocean of Sand: Libya is home to one of the most stunning parts of the Sahara Desert. It's not just a little sandbox, but an epic expanse of golden dunes that stretch as far as the eye can see. It's like nature's own sea of sand, minus the water and the fish, of course. But who needs water when you have camels?

Leptis Magna: Rome Away From Rome: Ever wanted to see Rome but found yourself in Libya? No problem! Visit Leptis Magna, one of the best-preserved Roman cities in the Mediterranean. It's like ancient Rome decided to take a vacation and forgot to leave. Walking through its ruins, you might expect to bump into a toga-wearing local!

Olive Oil Galore: In Libya, olive oil isn't just for cooking; it's a way of life. They love it so much that it's almost like a national drink. Libyan olive oil is to Libyans what maple syrup is to Canadians. So, don't be surprised if you see someone using it more liberally than sunscreen at the beach!

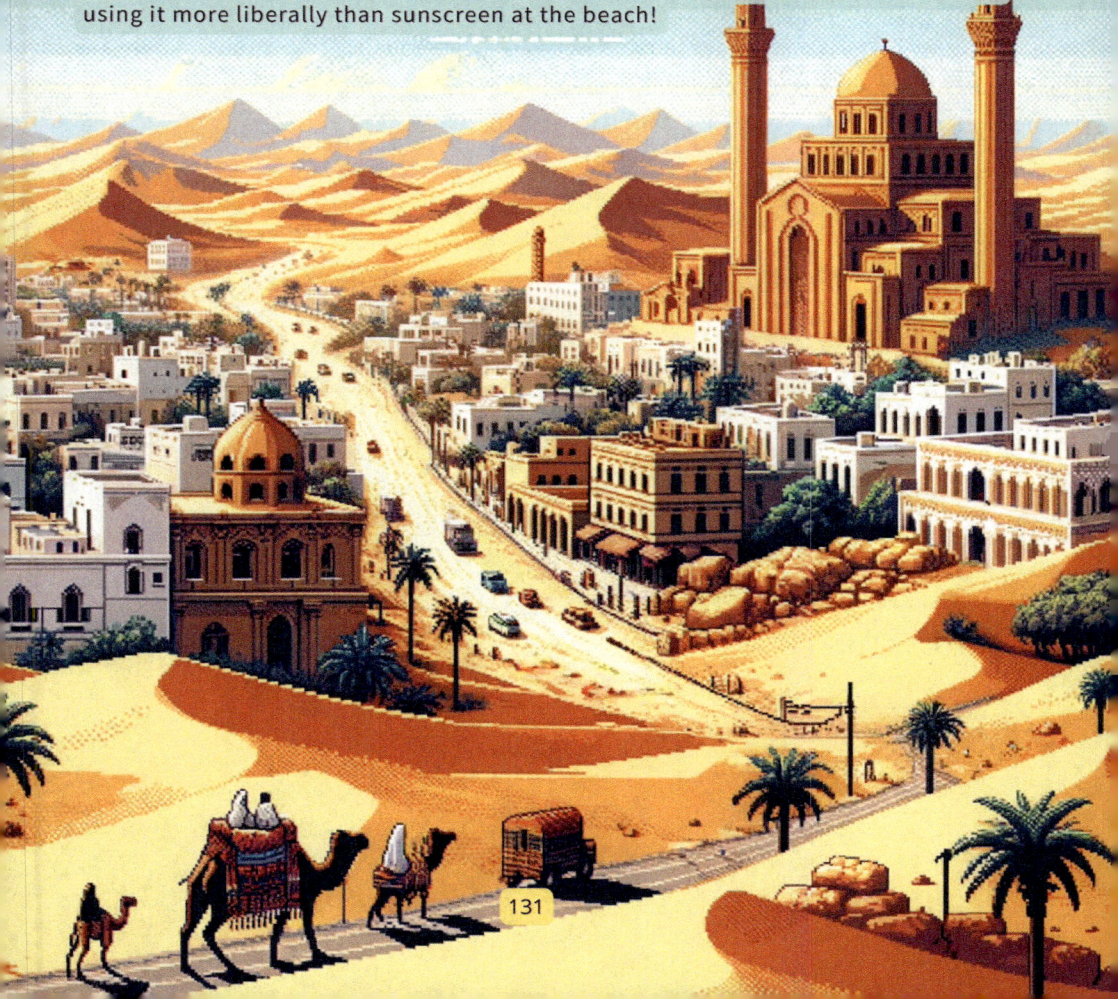

LIECHTENSTEIN

Western Europe
population: 39,584
Size (sq miles): 62
Size (sq km): 160

Tiny But Mighty: Liechtenstein is so small, you could blink and almost miss it! It's only 25 kilometers long – that's like running a half marathon with a bit extra for warm-up. But don't let its size fool you. This tiny country is packed with charm, mountains, and more stamps and banks than you'd expect in such a small place.

Rent-a-Country: Ever wanted to rule a country? In Liechtenstein, you can (kind of)! You can actually rent the whole country for a night. Yes, the entire country! It's like having the ultimate sleepover, but with a whole nation as your playground. People of Liechtenstein will stay in their home, of course, but you will have a lot of places just to yourself. Just imagine the game of hide and seek you could play!

Castle in the Clouds: Liechtenstein's Vaduz Castle isn't just a castle; it's a royal residence that looks like it's straight out of a fairy tale. Perched on a hill, it watches over the capital like a stern but kind grandparent. You can't visit the inside (because the royal family lives there), but just seeing it from the outside is like spotting Cinderella's castle without the theme park lines.

LITHUANIA

Eastern Europe • Baltic States
population: 2,870,191
Size (sq miles): 25,200
Size (sq km):   65,300

Basketball Fever: In Lithuania, basketball is huge. They love it so much, you'd think the national bird is a basketball! (It's not, btw). When the national team plays, the whole country turns into a sea of green and gold, and cheering for the team is like a national duty. It's said that babies learn to dribble before they walk!
Vilnius: The Baroque Beauty: The capital city, Vilnius, is like a giant outdoor art gallery, boasting one of the largest collections of Baroque architecture in Europe. Walking through Vilnius is like time-traveling to a grand, opulent past, but with way better Wi-Fi.
The Singing Revolution: Lithuanians are not just good at basketball; they're also great at singing. In the late 1980s, they sang their way to freedom during the Singing Revolution. It's like they used their voices as superpowers to change history. Imagine solving problems by starting a giant sing-along. If only all conflicts could be resolved with a good song!

LUXEMBOURG

Western Europe
population: 660,809
Size (sq miles): 998.6
Size (sq km): 2,586.4

Castle Galore: In Luxembourg, they love their castles so much, it seems they decided to put one around every corner. With over 50 castles and picturesque ruins, it's like the country is playing a real-life game of "King of the Castle". If you're a fan of medieval times, Luxembourg is your ultimate playground – just minus the dragons and knights!

Rich in More Ways Than One: Luxembourg might be small, but its wallet isn't. Known for being one of the wealthiest countries, it's like the tiny nation decided to show the world that size really doesn't matter when it comes to your bank account. It's the place where even the piggy banks need to go on a diet!

Tongue Twisters: In Luxembourg, speaking one language is so mainstream. People here usually speak at least three languages: Luxembourgish, French, and German. It's like living in a linguistic blender. Kids in Luxembourg probably play Scrabble in three different languages for fun!

MACAU
China

East Asia
population: 672,800
Size (sq miles): 44.5
Size (sq km):   115.3

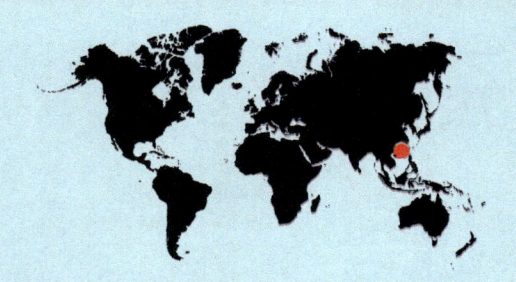

The Vegas of the East: Macau is often called the 'Vegas of the East', but it actually earns more in its casinos than Vegas does! It's like Vegas went on a vacation to Asia and decided to stay permanently. Here, the neon lights don't just shine; they practically dance, and the casinos aren't just buildings; they're like glittering palaces of luck and fortune.

A Bridge Not Too Far: Macau is connected to the mainland China by the world's longest sea-crossing bridge. This engineering marvel is so long (55 kilometers!), it's like they wanted to make sure even the people in the back seats of the car get to enjoy the view before reaching the other side.

Egg Tarts Galore: Macau loves its Portuguese-style egg tarts so much, they're practically a symbol of the city. With their flaky crust and creamy custard, it's like a tiny party in your mouth with every bite. They say you haven't really been to Macau until you've had an egg tart. It's the perfect snack after a long walk – or a long sit at the slot machines!

MADAGASCAR

Africa · Indian Ocean
population: 28,812,195
Size (sq miles): 228,880
Size (sq km):   592,796

Lemur Limbo: Madagascar is the world headquarters of lemurs, those cute, wide-eyed primates. They're found only here, making the island a giant lemur party! Some of them, like the Sifaka, are known for their funky 'dancing' as they move across the ground. It's like nature's own version of a dance-off, and the lemurs are the undisputed champions.

Tree Spikes Galore: Ever seen a forest of spiky trees? Madagascar's Avenue of the Baobabs is like a gathering of nature's giants, with huge, spiky trees lining the road. These trees look like they're straight out of a fantasy movie, standing tall and proud, showing off their hundreds of years of growth. It's like walking through a natural cathedral, only spikier!

Vanilla is the New Gold: Madagascar is one of the world's largest producers of vanilla, and they take their vanilla very seriously. It's like gold, but tastier! The scent of vanilla is so common, it's like the island has its own natural perfume. A visit to Madagascar might just leave you with a craving for vanilla-flavored everything!

MADEIRA
Portugal

Southern Europe - Atlantic
population: 250,769
Size (sq miles): 309
Size (sq km):   801

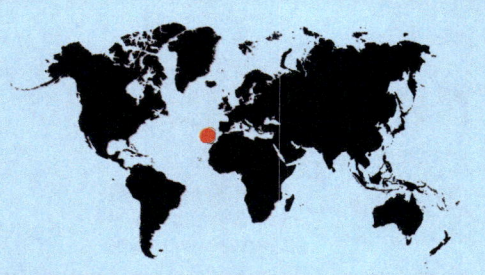

Basket Sled Rides: In Madeira, you can ride down steep streets in a wicker toboggan. Yes, that's right, a toboggan made of wicker, steered by two drivers called "carreiros". It's like a rollercoaster, but with baskets and without tracks. Fasten your seatbelts, or in this case, hold onto your hats!

Flower Power: Madeira is famous for its Flower Festival. Here, flowers aren't just in gardens; they're in parades! Imagine floats and costumes exploding in color, celebrating spring in the most vibrant way possible. It's like nature decided to throw its own fashion show.

The Age-Old Wine: Madeira wine is not just any wine; it's a wine that can last for over a century! This isn't the wine you forget at the back of the fridge; it's the kind you pass down like a precious family heirloom. Cheers to history in a bottle!

MALAWI

East Africa
population: 21,240,689
Size (sq miles): 45,747
Size (sq km):   118,484

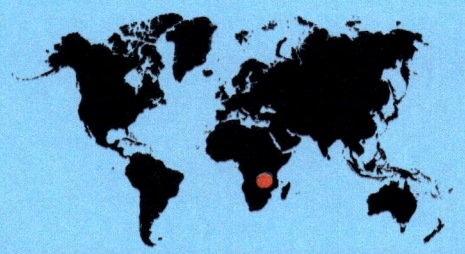

Lake of Stars: Malawi is home to Lake Malawi, also known as the "Lake of Stars." Explorer David Livingstone named it for the way fishermen's lanterns twinkled on the water at night, resembling a sky full of stars. It's like the lake decided to wear its own galaxy as a sparkly dress each night.

Chatty Drums and Dance: In Malawi, drums aren't just musical instruments; they're a way of communication. The traditional 'talking drums' can mimic the tones and rhythms of the local language. It's like sending a text message, but way more musical and you can dance to it.

The Fish That Throws a Festival: The Chambo fish is so popular in Malawi that it gets its own festival. It's like the fish are the celebrities of the lake, and the festival is their red carpet event. People celebrate with music, dance, and of course, lots of delicious Chambo dishes. Imagine being so famous as a fish that you get your own party!

MALAYSIA

Southeast Asia
population: 33,200,000
Size (sq miles): 127,724
Size (sq km):   330,803

Twin Tower Titans: Malaysia is famous for the Petronas Twin Towers in Kuala Lumpur. Once the tallest buildings in the world, they're like the twin superheroes of the skyline. Connected by a sky bridge, it's like they're holding hands – or maybe playing an epic game of rock-paper-scissors!

Rainforest Older than the Amazon: Malaysia's rainforests are ancient, even older than the Amazon! Walking through them is like stepping back in time, except with more bugs and less dinosaurs. These rainforests are home to some of the weirdest and wildest creatures you'll ever see – it's like nature's own fantasy novel.

Festival Fiesta: Malaysia is a cultural melting pot, and they celebrate just about everything. With Malay, Chinese, Indian, and indigenous groups, there's always a festival around the corner. It's like the country is always in party mode, with a never-ending supply of fireworks and delicious food. If there were a world championship for festivals, Malaysia would definitely be in the running!

MALDIVES

Indian Ocean
population: 515,132
Size (sq miles): 115
Size (sq km):   298

Island Hopping on Overdrive: The Maldives is made up of about 1,200 islands, so if you're into island hopping, this is your Olympic event! Each island is like a separate little world, some so small that you can walk across them in minutes. It's like the country is playing a game of "how many islands can we fit in the ocean?"

Underwater Cabinet Meetings: How about holding government meetings underwater? Yes, in 2009, the Maldives' cabinet did just that – equipped with scuba gear and a waterproof desk to highlight climate change's impact on their islands. It's like they took the term 'sinking feeling' in meetings quite literally!

Coconuts Aren't Just for Eating: In the Maldives, coconuts aren't just a tasty treat; they're a crafty resource. The locals are masters of coconut craftsmanship, turning them into everything from bowls to musical instruments. It's like every coconut is a potential piece of art or the next big hit in the coconut jazz band!

MALI

West Africa
population: 21,359,722
Size (sq miles): 479,245
Size (sq km): 1,241,238

Timbuktu: THE exotic place: Timbuktu in Mali is real, not just a mythical place in storybooks! Once a bustling hub of African learning and culture, it's home to ancient manuscripts and mosques made of mud. It's like a giant sandbox, but with more history and fewer sandcastles.

Musical Might: Mali is a powerhouse of African music, with world-famous musicians like Ali Farka Touré. Their music isn't just for entertainment; it's like a history lesson you can dance to. In Mali, a 'griot' is a musician-storyteller who keeps the history alive through songs. Think of them as the rock stars of history class!

The River Hippo Respect: The Niger River in Mali is home to hippos, which are treated with great respect and even a bit of fear. Locals consider them sacred and believe they bring good luck (as long as you keep a safe distance!). It's like the hippos are the unofficial mayors of the river - big, in charge, and worthy of respect.

MALTA

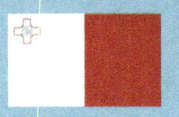

Southern Europe
population: 519,562
Size (sq miles): 122
Size (sq km): 316

Ancient Megaliths Galore: Malta might be small, but it's packed with some of the oldest free-standing structures in the world. The Ħaġar Qim and Mnajdra temples are older than the pyramids of Egypt! It's like Malta was the original trendsetter in ancient architecture – they were building epic monuments before it was cool.

Hollywood's Favorite Island: Malta is a bit of a movie star. It's been the backdrop for films like 'Gladiator' and TV shows like 'Game of Thrones'. With its stunning landscapes and ancient buildings, it's like Malta is constantly auditioning for Hollywood. Don't be surprised if you stumble onto a film set while wandering around!

Fiesta Fanatics: Maltese people love a good 'festa' – village festivals celebrating patron saints with fireworks, food, and music. It's like every village is in a friendly competition to throw the best party. Think of it as a series of block parties, but with more fireworks and saints.

MARSHALL ISLANDS

Oceania
population: 42,418
Size (sq miles): 70.05
Size (sq km):   181.43

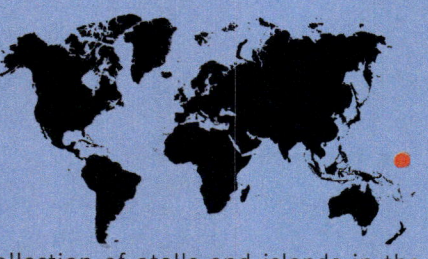

Atoll Allure: The Marshall Islands are a collection of atolls and islands in the Pacific Ocean. What's an atoll, you ask? It's like a necklace of tiny islands and coral reefs, hugging a beautiful lagoon. The country has over 1,000 of these little islands, so if you're playing a game of 'count the islands,' you might be here a while!

Dive into History: Below the waves, the Marshall Islands hold secrets of World War II – sunken ships and planes rest on the ocean floor. It's like an underwater museum, but instead of paintings, you get shipwrecks and fish swimming through history.

Navigating with Sticks: Forget Google Maps, the Marshallese once used stick charts for navigation. These charts, made of sticks and shells, weren't taken on voyages but studied and memorized beforehand. It's like having a map in your head, but way cooler and definitely more eco-friendly!

MARTINIQUE
France

Carribbean
population: 349,925
Size (sq miles): 436
Size (sq km): 1,128

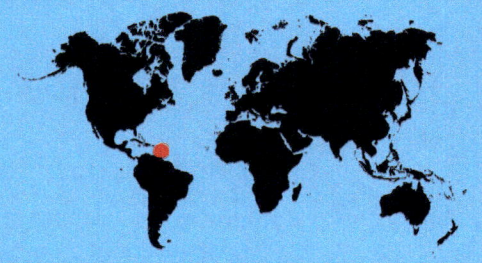

A Volcano with a Past: Martinique is famous for Mount Pelée, the volcano that once got a bit too fiery. In 1902, it erupted and wiped out the city of Saint-Pierre, then known as the "Paris of the Caribbean." Today, it's calm and a favorite spot for hikers. It's like the volcano said, "Oops, my bad," and decided to take a long nap.

Garden of Eden, Island Style: The Balata Gardens in Martinique are like stepping into a botanical dream. With over 3,000 species of tropical plants and flowers, it's like nature decided to show off. The garden even has a treetop walkway, because why just walk among flowers when you can walk above them?

Zouk: The Rhythm of the Island: Martinique is the birthplace of Zouk music, a fast-paced rhythm that makes it impossible to stand still. It's like the island has its own heartbeat, and it's set to dance mode. If you're in Martinique and your feet start moving on their own, blame it on the Zouk!

MAURITANIA

Africa
population: 4,244,878
Size (sq miles): 400,000
Size (sq km):   1,030,000

The Iron Railway: Mauritania boasts the longest train in the world, and it's not for passengers – it's for iron ore. Stretching up to 3 kilometers, it's like a metal snake slithering through the Sahara. Some adventurous travelers hitch rides atop the ore, but it's definitely not your average scenic railway journey!

Chinguetti: A Desert Library: Deep in the Sahara, the ancient city of Chinguetti is home to medieval libraries filled with thousands of manuscripts. It's like a treasure trove of knowledge, surrounded by sand dunes. It's so remote and preserved, you half expect to find a genie in a bottle between the bookshelves.

A Coastline of Contrast: Mauritania's coastline is where the Sahara meets the Atlantic Ocean. Imagine endless sand dunes suddenly taking a deep dive into the ocean. It's a dramatic landscape shift, like nature suddenly decided to switch from a desert movie to a beach movie.

MAURITIUS

Indian Ocean
population: 1,265,475
Size (sq miles): 790
Size (sq km): 2,040

Home of the Dodo: Mauritius is famous for being the only home of the dodo bird, which sadly went extinct in the 17th century. The dodo became the poster bird for "Oops, we shouldn't have done that." Today, it's a symbol of the island and a reminder to take better care of our feathery friends.

Sega Dance: The Rhythmic Heartbeat: In Mauritius, the Sega dance is a big deal. It started with the island's African slaves as a form of expression and has become a joyful, vibrant dance. It's like the island's version of a group hug, but with more rhythm and less awkwardness.

Underwater Waterfall Illusion: Off the coast of Mauritius, there's what looks like an underwater waterfall, but it's actually an optical illusion created by sand and silt runoff. It's nature's version of a magic trick. You have to see it from above to believe it – or not believe it!

MAYOTTE
France

Africa · Indian Ocean
population: 320,901
Size (sq miles): 144
Size (sq km):   374

The Lagoon of Legends: Mayotte boasts one of the largest enclosed lagoons in the world. It's so big, you could fit a small country in it! Surrounded by a double barrier reef, it's like nature's version of a VIP section in a club – exclusive and full of colorful marine life.

Ylang-Ylang: The Scent of Paradise: This small island is a big player in the world of perfumes, thanks to the Ylang-Ylang tree. Its flowers are used to make essential oils that smell like a tropical dream. Walking around Mayotte is like wandering through nature's own perfumery.

Lemurs Love to Leap: Mayotte might be part of France, but it has its own version of monkeys – the lemurs! These playful creatures are found in the island's forests and are known for their acrobatic jumps. They're like the island's own cheerleading squad, always ready to put on a show.

MEXICO

North America
population: 129,875,529
Size (sq miles): 761,610
Size (sq km):   1,972,550

Day of the Dead: A Lively Affair: In Mexico, the Day of the Dead (Día de Muertos) is a festival where skulls are colorful, and the mood is festive. It's when Mexicans remember their loved ones who've passed away with bright decorations and sweet skull-shaped candies. It's like a party where even the ancestors don't want to miss out!

Chili in Everything: In Mexico, they believe that if it's not spicy, it's not worth eating. Even their candies are spiked with chili! It's like a culinary roller coaster – thrilling, a bit scary, but totally worth the ride. Don't be surprised if you find yourself reaching for water more than you thought!

The Dance of the Flyers: Ever seen people spinning from a pole, high in the sky? In Mexico, this is the traditional 'Danza de los Voladores', or the Dance of the Flyers. Five men climb a 30-meter pole; four of them leap and spin down tied with ropes, while the fifth plays music on top. It's like a mix of a concert and a skydiving event, but without the parachutes!

MICRONESIA

Oceania
population: 104,468
Size (sq miles): 271
Size (sq km): 702

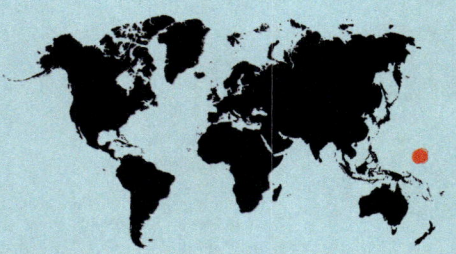

Islands Galore: Micronesia is like a giant scatter cushion of islands thrown across the Pacific Ocean. With over 600 islands, it's like nature was playing a game of "Let's see how many islands we can fit in here!" Each island is a tiny paradise with its own charm – it's like having 600 different flavors of tropical bliss.

Giant Stone Coins: In the island of Yap, money rocks – literally! They use giant stone disks called Rai stones as currency. Some are as big as cars! It's like their version of a bank account, but you definitely can't fit these in your wallet. Imagine trying to make change for one of those!

Navigating by the Stars: Forget GPS, the Micronesians are master star navigators. They've been using the stars, wind, and ocean currents to hop between islands for centuries. It's like they have a natural GPS built into their brains. Who needs Google Maps when you have the night sky?

MOLDOVA

Eastern Europe
population: 2,512,758
Size (sq miles): 13,067
Size (sq km): 33,843

Vineyards as Far as the Eye Can See: Moldova takes its wine seriously. So seriously, in fact, that it has more vineyards per square mile than any other country. It's like the entire country decided to throw a grape-growing party and everyone – and every field – showed up!

A Cellar Like No Other: Ever wanted to visit the world's largest wine cellar? Head to Mileștii Mici in Moldova, where the cellar stretches over 200 kilometers! It's so big; you need a car to tour it. It's like they took "wine road trip" quite literally. Don't worry, there are no speed limits, just endless rows of wine.

The Epicenter of Epic Parties: The Moldovans don't just party; they throw 'sărbătoarea' – village feasts that make regular parties look like quiet get-togethers. With music, dancing, and, of course, plenty of wine, these celebrations can last for days. It's like the whole village hits the 'celebrate' button and forgets where the 'off' switch is.

MONACO

Western Europe
population: 39,050
Size (sq miles): 0.80
Size (sq km): 2.08

A Country You Can Walk Across: Monaco is so small, you can walk across the entire country in just over an hour! It's like the whole country is a cozy neighborhood where everyone knows everyone (or at least knows of them). Imagine telling your friends you walked across an entire country during lunch break!

Formula One in the Streets: The Monaco Grand Prix turns the city streets into a high-speed race track. It's like Monaco's version of fast and furious, but with more yachts and celebrities. The race is known for its tight corners, making it a thrilling (and slightly hair-raising) event for both drivers and spectators.

The Palace on the Rock: Monaco's Prince's Palace sits on a rock overlooking the sea, like a scene from a fairy tale. The changing of the guard ceremony is a daily attraction. It's like the royal guards are putting on a show – "Guarding the Palace: The Musical," but with less singing and more marching.

MONGOLIA

East Asia
population: 3,227,863
Size (sq miles): 603,909
Size (sq km): 1,564,116

Nomadic by Nature: In Mongolia, many people still live a nomadic lifestyle. It's like they've taken "working from home" to a whole new level – their homes (yurts) and their office (the great outdoors) move with them! Imagine changing your address as often as you change your clothes.

The Singing Dunes: The Gobi Desert in Mongolia is home to the 'singing sands' at the Khongoryn Els. When the wind blows, the sand dunes hum a tune. It's like nature's own playlist, but you can't skip tracks, and the volume control is basically the weather.

Naadam: The Nomad Olympics: Mongolia's Naadam Festival is like the Olympics, but with more horses and archery. It showcases the 'Three Manly Sports': horse racing, archery, and wrestling. The wrestlers wear colorful outfits and have eagle dances – because in Mongolia, even wrestling has flair!

MONTENEGRO

Europe · Balkans
population: 633.158
Size (sq miles): 5,333
Size (sq km): 13,812

Mountains That Touch the Sky: In Montenegro, it's all about the mountains. They're so tall and majestic, it's like they're trying to high-five the clouds. These mountains aren't just for looking at; they're a playground for hikers, bikers, and anyone who enjoys a good "wow" moment with nature.

Kotor: A Medieval Maze: The old town of Kotor feels like a step back in time. With its winding streets and ancient walls, it's like a medieval labyrinth, but instead of a minotaur, you find cozy cafes and curious cats. It's a history lesson you can walk through, and every corner is a new chapter.

Breakfast: A Feast Fit for a King: In Montenegro, breakfast isn't just the first meal of the day; it's a feast. Imagine a table groaning under plates of cured meats, cheeses, fresh bread, and pastries. It's like they believe in starting the day with a party on your plate. Who needs alarm clocks when you have breakfast like this?

MONTSERRAT
United Kingdom

Carribbean
population: 4,390
Size (sq miles): 39
Size (sq km): 102

The Volcano That Reshaped an Island: Montserrat is known for its Soufrière Hills Volcano. In the 1990s, it woke up and decided to remodel the island, covering the capital city in ash. It's like the volcano said, "I think this place needs a makeover," but took it a bit too far. Today, the volcano is a big tourist attraction - because who doesn't want to see Mother Nature's own redecoration work?

The Emerald Isle of the Caribbean: Montserrat is known as the 'Emerald Isle' of the Caribbean, thanks to its Irish heritage. Yes, you read that right – Irish! It's the only country outside Ireland where St. Patrick's Day is a public holiday. It's like Ireland and the Caribbean had a baby, and it turned out to be an island!

Music in the Air: This island loves its music, especially calypso and soca. The annual Calypso Monarch competition is a big deal. It's like "Montserrat's Got Talent," but everyone's competing to be the Calypso King or Queen. The island rhythm is so contagious; you might find yourself dancing before you even realize it!

MOROCCO

North Africa
population: 37,984,655
Size (sq miles): 172,300
Size (sq km):   446,300

Souks: Where Bargains and Banter Collide: In Morocco's souks (markets), haggling is not just a skill; it's an art form. It's like a sport where the ball is a beautiful rug or a shiny lantern, and your words are your play moves. Walk through a souk, and you'll find a kaleidoscope of colors, smells, and the friendliest arguments you've ever heard!

The Atlas Mountains: The Atlas Mountains in Morocco aren't just a range; they're like the backbone of the land. They stretch majestically across the country, offering breathtaking views and hiking adventures. It's like nature's own version of a stairway to heaven, but with more goats.

Mint Tea: The National Drink: In Morocco, mint tea is more than a beverage; it's a sign of hospitality. Refusing it is like saying no to a hug. It's served super sweet and poured from high above to create a frothy top. It's part performance, part refreshment – the Moroccan way of saying, "Welcome, let's chat!"

MOZAMBIQUE

Southern Africa
population: 34,173,805
Size (sq miles): 309,500
Size (sq km): 801,590

Beaches That Stretch Forever: In Mozambique, the beaches seem to go on forever, like nature's own version of an endless runner game. With over 2,500 kilometers of coastline, you could walk along the beach and feel like you're on a never-ending holiday. It's the perfect spot for anyone who loves sand between their toes and a sea breeze in their hair!

The Maputo Railway Station: A Star of Its Own: The Maputo Railway Station isn't just a place to catch a train; it's a work of art. Some say Gustave Eiffel, the man behind the Eiffel Tower, had a hand in its design. It's like the train station decided to dress up as a historical monument and ended up stealing the show!

The Magical Sound of the Timbila: Mozambique is home to the timbila, a traditional musical instrument. Part of the xylophone family, it's made entirely from local materials. It's like the trees and gourds got together to form a band. The sound is so unique it even has a spot on UNESCO's list of Masterpieces of the Oral and Intangible Heritage of Humanity.

MYANMAR

Southeast Asia
population: 57,526,449
Size (sq miles): 261,229
Size (sq km):   676,579

Shwedagon Pagoda: The Golden Giant: In Myanmar, the Shwedagon Pagoda isn't just a monument; it's a colossal treasure chest. Covered in gold and studded with diamonds, it's like the pagoda is dressed up for the fanciest party ever, and everyone's invited. Standing at 99 meters tall, it's a beacon of shimmer and shine that can be seen from miles away.

Inle Lake's Leg-Rowing Fishermen: The fishermen of Inle Lake have a unique style of rowing – they use their legs! It's like they decided that using arms was too mainstream. Balancing on one leg and wrapping the other around the oar, they glide across the lake with a grace that would make a ballet dancer envious.

Thanaka: The Natural Sunscreen: In Myanmar, wearing Thanaka is a tradition. This yellowish-white cosmetic paste, made from ground bark, is worn for sun protection and beauty. It's like having an all-natural makeup and sunscreen in one, often applied in lovely patterns. Who needs fancy creams when you've got Thanaka?

NAMIBIA

Southern Africa
population: 2,777,232
Size (sq miles): 318,772
Size (sq km): 825,615

Dunes that Touch the Sky: In Namibia, the sand dunes are so big they make mountains look like molehills. The star is Dune 7, the highest in the country, standing tall at over 380 meters. It's like nature's own skyscraper, but made of sand and without the elevators. Climbing it feels like joining an exclusive club – the "I conquered a mountain of sand" club.

Skeleton Coast: The Shipwreck Museum of the Atlantic: The Skeleton Coast is like a graveyard for ships, with bones of old ships peeking out of the sand. It's as if the sea decided to start its own outdoor museum but forgot to hire a curator. This eerie coastline offers a ghostly beauty that's strangely captivating.

Cape Cross Seal Colony: At Cape Cross, you'll find a seal colony where the seals lounge more than the laziest beach-goers. With over 100,000 seals, it's like a concert crowd, but smellier and with more napping. They're the true celebrities of the Namibian coast, drawing tourists from all over the world.

NAURU

Oceania
population: 10,834
Size (sq miles): 8.1
Size (sq km):   21

The Birdman of Nauru: In Nauru, there's a legend about a giant bird called the Tebwi. It's said that this massive bird could carry off a grown man. Today, while you might not find the Tebwi, you'll definitely find a nation in love with storytelling. It's like their version of a blockbuster movie, but in legend form.

A National Passion for Weightlifting: Forget football or cricket; in Nauru, weightlifting is the national sport. It seems like everyone's either lifting weights or cheering for someone who does. It's the kind of place where "Do you even lift, bro?" isn't just a question; it's a way of life.

Coconut Galore: Coconuts are to Nauru what potatoes are to Idaho. They're everywhere, and they're used for everything – from food to traditional medicine. It's like the Swiss Army knife of the tropics. If Nauruans could build houses out of coconuts, they probably would!

NEPAL

South Asia
population: 30,666,598
Size (sq miles): 56,956
Size (sq km): 147,516

The Top of the World: Nepal is home to Mount Everest, the tallest mountain on Earth. It's so high (8,848 meters or more than 29000 feet!) that it's like the earth is reaching up to get a better view of the stars. Climbing it is on many people's bucket lists, right between "Learn to play the guitar" and "Become a ninja", though it might well the hardest and most dangerous of the three.

Kumari: The Living Goddess: In Nepal, they don't just worship deities in temples; they have a living goddess, the Kumari. She's a young girl chosen to be the goddess until she hits puberty. It's like being a divine version of a child celebrity, but with more rituals and fewer paparazzi.

Namaste, The Long Way: In Nepal, people have really long names. It's not uncommon to meet someone with a name as long as a sentence. It's like parents decide to give their child's entire autobiography in their name. So, when you say "Namaste" to someone, make sure you have a few extra seconds!

NETHERLANDS

Europe
population: 17,680,000
Size (sq miles): 16,040
Size (sq km):   41,543

Biking Bonanza: In the Netherlands, bikes might just outnumber people! This flat country is crazy about cycling. There are more bikes than residents, and in cities like Amsterdam, bike traffic jams can happen. Imagine a world where your biggest traffic worry is a slow-pedaling grandma!

The King's Birthday Bash: Every year on April 27th, the Netherlands turns into an orange sea for King's Day, celebrating the king's birthday. People wear orange everything - hats, shirts, even orange hair! There are street parties, flea markets, and boat parades. It's like the entire country is having one giant, orange-themed birthday party.

Tiny Country, Giant Contributions: Did you know the Netherlands is a bit of a superhero in the world of inventions? They gave us the microscope, the telescope, and even orange carrots! Originally, carrots were purple, white, and yellow, but 17th-century Dutch farmers bred them to be orange. Why? Well, some say it was to honor the royal family, the House of Orange. Imagine changing the color of a veggie just for national pride!

NEW CALEDONIA

France

Oceania
population: 289,000
Size (sq miles): 7,172
Size (sq km): 18,575

Heart-Shaped Natural Wonder: In New Caledonia, there's a heart you can see from the sky! The Heart of Voh is a natural formation of mangroves that have grown into the shape of a heart. It's like nature's own love letter, best viewed from a plane or a hilltop. Who knew mangroves were such romantics?

Kanak Culture: The Kanak people, New Caledonia's indigenous inhabitants, have a rich culture that's over 3,000 years old. One unique aspect is the Grand Hut, a special large hut used for community gatherings. Imagine having a house just for parties – now that's thinking ahead!

Nickel Riches: This island is more than just pretty beaches; it's sitting on a treasure trove of nickel! In fact, New Caledonia is one of the world's largest producers of nickel. So, if you're walking around and find a shiny rock, you might just have stumbled upon a piece of the island's wealth.

NEW ZEALAND

Oceania
population: 5,112,000
Size (sq miles): 103,483
Size (sq km): 268,021

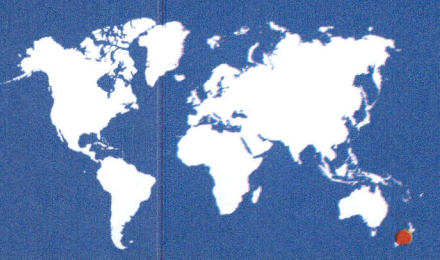

Birds that Forgot to Fly: Ever heard of a bird that can't fly? Welcome to New Zealand, home of the Kiwi bird, which seems to have skipped flying lessons. These little birds prefer strolling through the forests and have become a national symbol. Maybe they just enjoy the scenic route!

Southern Lights Spectacular: In New Zealand, you can catch the Aurora Australis, also known as the Southern Lights. It's like the famous Northern Lights, but for the cool kids in the Southern Hemisphere. Imagine seeing the sky dance in colors while you're chilling in the world's adventure capital!

Hobbit Homes: Ever wanted to visit The Shire from "The Lord of the Rings"? In New Zealand, you can! The movie set still exists, complete with hobbit holes and the Green Dragon Inn. It's like stepping into a fantasy world, minus the dragons and orcs, thankfully.

NICARAGUA

Central America
population: 6,702,000
Size (sq miles): 50,337
Size (sq km): 130,373

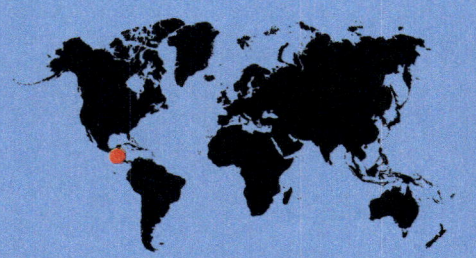

Land of Lakes and Volcanoes: Nicaragua is known as the land of lakes and volcanoes. It's got 19 volcanoes, some of which you can even sandboard down! Imagine surfing down the side of a volcano. Talk about an extreme sport!

Giant Lake Island: In Lake Nicaragua, there's a huge island called Ometepe, formed by two volcanoes. It's like nature decided to play a game of "volcanic island in the middle of a lake." And yes, you can climb those volcanoes for a breathtaking view.

Baseball Love: While most of Latin America is crazy about football (soccer), Nicaraguans prefer baseball. It's the national sport! Don't be surprised if you see more baseball fields than soccer fields. It's like their own version of the World Series, every game!

NIGER

West Africa
population: 25,130,000
Size (sq miles): 489,191
Size (sq km):   1,267,000

A Festival for Camels: In Niger, there's a festival called the Cure Salée, or "Festival of the Nomads." It's basically a huge party for nomadic tribes, and camels get dressed up too! Imagine camels in beauty contests and camel races. It's like the Kentucky Derby, but with humps!

The Wodaabe's Charm Dance: The Wodaabe tribe in Niger has a unique courtship ritual. Men wear elaborate makeup and costumes to perform the Yaake dance, trying to charm potential wives. It's like a beauty pageant where the guys are the contestants!

A City Half as Old as Time: The city of Agadez, with its stunning mud-brick architecture, dates back to the 11th century. It's so old, it's like walking through a live history book. The city's centerpiece is a towering minaret, standing as a testament to ancient architectural wonders.

NIGERIA

Africa
population: 216,746,934
Size (sq miles): 356,669
Size (sq km):   923,768

Nollywood Stars: Nigeria's film industry, affectionately called Nollywood, is the second-largest in the world by volume, just after Bollywood and before Hollywood. It's like Hollywood, but with more drama, more action, and way more creative budget solutions. In Nollywood, a little imagination turns a backyard into an epic movie set!

The Giant of Africa: Nigeria is often nicknamed the "Giant of Africa" due to its large population and economy. It's like the big brother of African countries, bustling with over 200 million people. In Lagos, the largest city, the energy is so high it makes New York seem like a sleepy town!

Land of Butterflies: Nigeria is a haven for butterflies, boasting one of the largest diversities of these colorful creatures in the world. It's like Mother Nature decided to throw a butterfly party and everyone's invited. Walking through some Nigerian forests is like stepping into a real-life fairy tale, just without the talking animals!

NIUE

Oceania
population: 1,520
Size (sq miles): 100
Size (sq km):   260

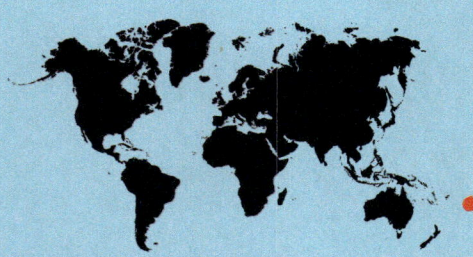

The World's First Wi-Fi Nation: Niue was the first country to offer free Wi-Fi to all its residents and visitors. It's like the island said, "Data plans? We don't need no data plans!" In Niue, staying connected is as easy as enjoying the sunshine - which is also plentiful!

The "Rock" of Polynesia: Known as "The Rock" of Polynesia, Niue isn't your typical sandy beach paradise. It's a large upraised coral atoll, making it one of the world's largest coral islands. This means you can go exploring in caves and chasms instead of building sandcastles. It's adventure mode, island style!

Non-Venomous Snake-Free Zone: Here's a fun fact for the snake-averse: Niue is one of the few places in the world without any snakes. That's right, zero slithery friends. It's like the island declared, "No snakes on this plane... or island!" So, you can walk through the lush forests without worrying about any surprise hissing guests.

NORTH KOREA

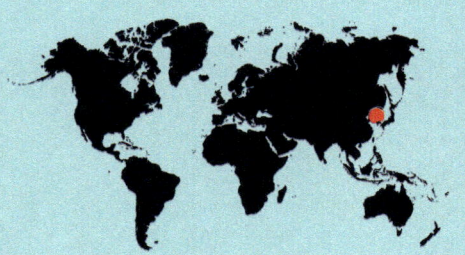

East Asia
population: 25,981,000
Size (sq miles): 46,540
Size (sq km): 120,538

Pyongyang's Traffic Ladies: In the capital city, Pyongyang, instead of traffic lights, elegantly dressed traffic ladies control the flow. They're selected for their looks and are almost as iconic as the city's monuments. It's like a highly choreographed roadside ballet, but with cars and buses.

Hotel of Doom: The Ryugyong Hotel in Pyongyang, also known as the "Hotel of Doom," is an unfinished 105-story pyramid-shaped skyscraper. It's been under construction since 1987 and is a bit of a local legend. It's like the Eiffel Tower of North Korea, only less iron and more mystery.

Mass Games Spectacle: North Korea is famous for its Mass Games, a spectacular display of gymnastics and artistic performances. Picture thousands of performers moving in perfect unison - it's like a human kaleidoscope. This event is designed to showcase national unity and is a sight to behold, blending artistry with a scale that's almost beyond belief.

NORTH MACEDONIA

Europe
population: 2,077,132
Size (sq miles): 9,928
Size (sq km): 25,713

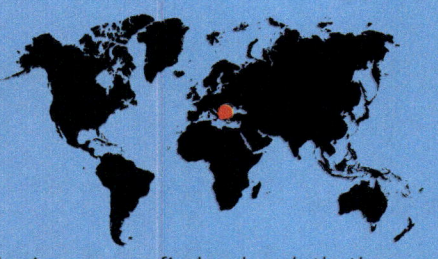

Land of Sunken Churches: In North Macedonia, you can find a church that's more underwater than over. The Church of St. Nicholas in Mavrovo Lake becomes submerged when the lake fills up. It's like they couldn't decide between building a church or a submarine!

Ohrid: A City of Two Halves: The city of Ohrid is not only one of Europe's oldest, but it's also split between the old and the new. Strolling through Ohrid is like time-traveling – one minute you're in a bustling modern café, and the next, you're walking along cobblestone streets lined with medieval architecture.

The Mystery of the Stone Dolls: In the village of Kuklica, you can find over 120 naturally formed stone pillars, known as the Stone Dolls. Legend has it they were wedding guests turned to stone by a jilted lover. It's like nature's own version of a fairy tale, but with less Prince Charming and more geology.

NORTHERN IRELAND
United Kingdom

Western Europe
population: 1,904,563
Size (sq miles): 5,530
Size (sq km):   14,330

Giant's Causeway: A Giant's Jigsaw Puzzle: The Giant's Causeway is a natural wonder made of about 40,000 interlocking basalt columns. Legend says it was built by a giant – which explains the name. It's like nature's version of LEGO, but with hexagonal pieces perfectly fitted together. Good luck trying to rearrange them, though!

Titanic's Birthplace: Belfast, the capital of Northern Ireland, is where the famous (and infamous) Titanic was built. It's like the city had its own giant baby, which then went off to make a big splash in the world, quite literally. They even have a museum shaped like an iceberg!

A Love for 'Craic': In Northern Ireland, if someone says they're having great 'craic', don't be puzzled. 'Craic' is an Irish term for fun or a good time. It's all about enjoying life, sharing stories, and having a laugh. So, in Northern Ireland, the craic is always 90 (which means really good)!

NORTHERN MARIANA ISLANDS

United States

Oceania
population: 57,216
Size (sq miles): 179
Size (sq km): 464

Golfing in an old War Zone: The Northern Mariana Islands have a golf course built around old World War II bunkers. It's not uncommon to hit a drive around old artillery. It's like playing a peaceful game of golf in the middle of history's leftovers!

The Forbidden Island: One of the islands, Pagan, is often called the Forbidden Island. It's been largely uninhabited since a volcanic eruption in the 1980s. Today, it's a surreal mix of lush jungle and volcanic landscapes – sort of like nature's version of a "Do Not Disturb" sign.

Chicken of the Trees: On the islands, coconut crabs are a common sight. These massive crabs can climb trees and crack open coconuts. They're like the local heavy-duty equipment for nature's toughest nuts. Watching a coconut crab at work is like seeing a real-life transformer in action, just slower and hungrier.

NORWAY

Northern Europe • Scandinavia
population: 5,425,270
Size (sq miles): 148,729
Size (sq km):   385,207

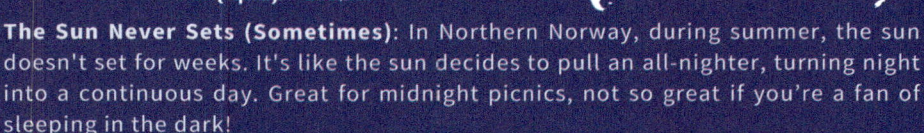

The Sun Never Sets (Sometimes): In Northern Norway, during summer, the sun doesn't set for weeks. It's like the sun decides to pull an all-nighter, turning night into a continuous day. Great for midnight picnics, not so great if you're a fan of sleeping in the dark!

Scream for Ice Cream: Norwegians love ice cream. They consume it en masse, even when it's cold outside, making them one of the top ice cream consumers per capita in the world. It's like they decided to chill with ice cream, regardless of the weather. Snow or shine, it's always ice cream time!

Tunnel Town: Norway is like the Swiss cheese of countries, with over 1,000 tunnels. The Laerdal Tunnel is the world's longest road tunnel, stretching 15 miles. It's like they took "digging a hole to China" seriously and just kept going. Driving through, you might wonder if you'll pop out on the other side of the world!

OMAN

Middle East
population: 5,223,000
Size (sq miles): 119,499
Size (sq km):   309,500

The Frankincense Trail: In Oman, frankincense isn't just for wise men in nativity plays. The country has an ancient history with the fragrant resin, boasting a trail of frankincense trees. It's like Oman decided to make air fresheners a national treasure!

Musandam Fjords: Norway of the Middle East: The Musandam Peninsula in Oman is known as the 'Norway of the Middle East' because of its beautiful fjords. With dramatic cliffs and crystal-clear waters, it's like nature's own version of a 3D movie, except the glasses are optional.

The Goat Market: In Nizwa, there's a lively goat market where locals haggle over goats like it's Black Friday. It's a bleating, bargaining bonanza, and possibly the only place where you might overhear, "This goat has great mileage and a smooth ride!"

PAKISTAN

South Asia
population: 235,824,860
Size (sq miles): 340,509
Size (sq km): 881,913

The High-Flying Peaks: Pakistan is home to some of the world's highest mountains, including K2, the second tallest after Everest. It's like the country saw other mountains and said, "Hold my chai, and watch this." For mountain enthusiasts, it's like visiting a celebrity gala, but with more snow and less red carpet.

The Ancient City of Mohenjo-Daro: In Pakistan lies one of the world's earliest major urban settlements, Mohenjo-Daro, dating back to 2500 BCE. It's like walking into a real-life history book, except the pages are made of bricks and ancient wisdom. Who needs a time machine when you have archeological sites?

A Love for Cricket: Cricket in Pakistan isn't just a sport; it's a national obsession. When there's a cricket match, streets go empty, and cheers can be heard from rooftops. It's like the whole country collectively holds its breath, only breathing out when there's a six or a wicket!

PALAU

Oceania
population: 18,094
Size (sq miles): 177
Size (sq km): 459

Jellyfish Lake: A Squishy Wonderland: In Palau, you can swim in Jellyfish Lake, filled with thousands of harmless jellyfish. It's like a giant, wobbly, underwater ball pit, but with jellyfish instead of plastic balls. Perfect for those who like their swims with a side of squish!

Rock Islands: Nature's Artwork: The Rock Islands of Palau are like a gallery of nature's sculptures, scattered across the ocean. These mushroom-shaped islets are covered in lush greenery and surrounded by crystal-clear waters. It's as if Mother Nature tried her hand at pottery and absolutely nailed it.

Giant Clams: The Heavyweights of the Sea: Palau's waters are home to some of the world's largest clams, big enough to make a mermaid's couch. These giant clams can weigh over 200 kilograms – that's like cuddling with a small piano! And with their vibrant colors, they're not just big; they're also fashion icons of the ocean.

PALESTINE

Middle East
population: 5,101,416
Size (sq miles): 2,402
Size (sq km): 6,220

Floating on the Dead Sea: The Dead Sea, bordering the West Bank, is so salty you can effortlessly float in it. It's like nature's own inflatable pool, but with healing properties and no need for floaties. Perfect for those who never mastered the art of swimming – just lie back and enjoy the natural buoyancy!

The Ancient Art of Olive Oil Making: Olive trees are abundant in the West Bank, and the tradition of olive oil production goes back thousands of years. It's like the region decided to become a master chef in oil-making. Visit during the harvest season, and you might just get roped into an olive-picking adventure – it's hands-on history!

A Town Painted in Murals – Bethlehem: The walls of Bethlehem are a canvas for local and international artists, including Banksy. Walking through the town is like visiting an open-air art gallery, with each mural telling a story. It's street art with a dose of history, a pinch of politics, and a whole lot of soul.

PANAMA

Central America
population: 4,381,579
Size (sq miles): 29,119
Size (sq km):   75,417

The Panama Canal: A Shortcut for Ships: The Panama Canal is like the world's greatest shortcut. It's an engineering marvel that allows ships to bypass the long and treacherous journey around South America. Imagine a water elevator, but for massive ships, saving them a 12,000-mile detour. It's the maritime equivalent of cutting in line, but with international permission!

The Pollera: A Dress with a Story: The Pollera, Panama's traditional dress, is an explosion of color, embroidery, and layers. It's so detailed that making one can take up to a year. Wearing a Pollera is like carrying a story – each color and stitch has a meaning. It's the ultimate conversation starter, but you might need a whole evening just for introductions.

A Birdwatcher's Paradise: Panama is home to more bird species than the United States and Canada combined. It's like the birds decided to have a convention and Panama was voted the best location. With over 970 species, birdwatching in Panama can feel like scrolling through an avian Instagram, but in real life and with more squawking.

PAPUA NEW GUINEA

Oceania
population: 9,119,010
Size (sq miles): 178,704
Size (sq km): 462,840

The Land of a Thousand Cultures: Papua New Guinea boasts over 800 languages, making it the most linguistically diverse place on Earth. It's like every village decided to make up its own language. Visiting different parts of the country might feel like flipping through a phrasebook on fast-forward.

The Sing-Sing Festivals: The Sing-Sing festivals are a riot of color, dance, and music, where tribes gather to show off their unique cultures. It's like a fashion show, but with feathers, face paint, and traditional beats. Imagine trying to coordinate an outfit when your next-door neighbor is from a totally different culture!

Birds of Paradise Galore: Papua New Guinea is home to most of the world's species of Birds of Paradise. These birds are so flashy and flamboyant, they make peacocks look modest. Birdwatching here is less about binoculars and more about witnessing a natural runway show in the rainforest.

PARAGUAY

South America
population: 7,353,672
Size (sq miles): 157,048
Size (sq km): 406,752

The Land of Impressive Water Power: Paraguay is home to the Itaipu Dam, one of the world's largest hydroelectric plants. It's like Paraguay and Brazil got together for a project and accidentally created a power monster. The amount of water that flows through here could fill a few Olympic-sized swimming pools every second – talk about a heavy flow day!

The Language Duo: Paraguay is a bilingual nation where almost everyone speaks both Spanish and Guarani. It's like everyone in the country decided to double up on languages just for fun. In Paraguay, saying hello is twice the fun, and you get to choose which language to use each time!

A country with a heart: Paraguay is smack-dab in the middle of South America, giving it the nickname "Corazón de América" or "Heart of America." It's not just a sweet name; it's geographically true! And like a true heart, it pumps a blend of cultures, heat, and passion throughout the continent. It's the love machine of South America, just with more yerba mate and sopa Paraguaya!

PERU

South America
population: 33,359,418
Size (sq miles): 496,225
Size (sq km): 1,285,216

Machu Picchu: The Stairmaster Challenge: Machu Picchu, the ancient Inca city, is nestled high in the Andes. Visiting is like taking on the world's most scenic Stairmaster. The breathtaking views come with a side of altitude and a whole lot of stairs. It's the ultimate workout with a historical twist!

The Nazca Lines: Ancient Doodles or Alien Art? In the Nazca desert, you'll find the mysterious Nazca Lines. These enormous geoglyphs are best seen from the sky and range from simple lines to intricate animal figures. It's like ancient Peruvians were trying to communicate with the gods, or maybe they just really liked big doodles.

Potato Paradise: Peru is the birthplace of the potato, with over 3,000 different varieties. It's like the country hit the potato jackpot. Here, you can have a different type of potato for every meal and still not try them all. It's the ultimate destination for carb lovers – potato paradise!

PHILIPPINES

Southeast Asia
population: 113,811,000
Size (sq miles): 115,831
Size (sq km): 300,000

More Islands Than Days in a Year: The Philippines boasts over 7,000 islands, which means you could visit a new island every day for almost 20 years! It's like nature's version of a buffet – you'll never run out of options, but deciding where to go next can be a real challenge.

Jeepneys: The Kings of the Road: Jeepneys are the most popular means of public transport in the Philippines. They started as military jeeps left by the Americans after World War II and were transformed into colorful, flamboyant buses. Riding a jeepney is like hopping onto a moving art piece – it's cheap, cheerful, and sometimes a little crowded!

The Sweetest Mangoes: The Philippines is known for having the sweetest mangoes in the world. The Carabao mango, in particular, is so sweet and juicy, it's like eating sunshine in fruit form. It's not just a mango; it's a national treasure that you can eat for dessert, breakfast, or just because!

PITCAIRN ISLAND
United Kingdom

Oceania - South Pacific
population: 50
Size (sq miles): 18
Size (sq km): 47

Tiny Population, Big Fame: Pitcairn Island is famous for its tiny population. With around 50 people, it's more like a small neighborhood than a country. Everyone knows everyone, and 'anonymous' is just a word in the dictionary. It's like living in a place where your next-door neighbor is also your mailman, grocer, and the mayor!

Descendants of Mutineers: The residents of Pitcairn are descendants of the Bounty mutineers and their Tahitian companions. It's like the island was founded on a real-life pirate drama, but with less swashbuckling and more gardening. Talk about a family tree with some interesting roots!

Unique Pitcairn Language: The island has its own language, Pitkern, a mix of 18th-century English and Tahitian. It's like the islanders created their own secret code, but instead of spies, they're just chatting about the weather and what's for lunch. If you visit, get ready for a linguistic adventure as unique as the island itself!

POLAND

Eastern Europe
population: 37,797,005
Size (sq miles): 120,726
Size (sq km):   312,679

The Moving Capital: Poland's capital has been a bit of a traveler. It moved from Gniezno to Krakow and finally to Warsaw. It's like the country couldn't decide where to settle down. Maybe next, it'll swipe right on a completely new city!

The Land of Salted Wonders: The Wieliczka Salt Mine is a marvel, with chapels, chandeliers, and sculptures all carved out of rock salt. It's like the miners were part-time artists, or maybe they just really liked playing with their food.

A Sweet Tooth for History: In Poland, gingerbread isn't just a treat; it's a piece of history. Toruń gingerbread has been around since the Middle Ages. It's like baking a cookie and ending up with a historical artifact – delicious and educational!

PORTUGAL

Southern Europe
population: 10,295,000
Size (sq miles): 35,603
Size (sq km): 92,212

The Age of Discoveries Never Ended: Portugal kicked off the Age of Discoveries, and it seems like they never really stopped. From Vasco da Gama to Fernando Magellan, Portuguese explorers were the original travel bloggers, but with ships instead of Instagram.

A Sweet Tooth for Tiles: Azulejos, the decorative tiles seen all over Portugal, aren't just for show. They tell stories, decorate homes, and even help keep buildings cool. It's like Portugal decided wallpapers were too mainstream and went for something a bit more... ceramic.

The Land of Cork Trees: Portugal is the world's largest producer of cork. They have so many cork trees; it's like they can play a never-ending game of 'stop the bottle.' Walking through a cork forest in Portugal might just make you feel like you've stepped into a giant bulletin board!

PUERTO RICO
United States

Carribbean
population: 3,194,000
Size (sq miles): 3,515
Size (sq km):   9,104

Bioluminescent Bays: Nature's Nightlights: Puerto Rico is home to three of the world's few bioluminescent bays. At night, these waters light up with glowing microorganisms, creating a natural light show. It's like the sea decided to throw its own rave party, and plankton are the disco lights!

The Coquí Symphony: The coquí frog is a tiny but mighty symbol of Puerto Rico. Their loud, distinct 'ko-KEE' chorus at night is like the island's soundtrack. It's nature's way of saying, "Who needs Spotify when you've got these little guys?"

The Observatory That Reached for the Stars: The Arecibo Observatory was one of the world's largest radio telescopes, nestled in the hills of Puerto Rico. It was so big, it made your satellite dish look like a toy. For years, it listened to the whispers of the universe, until it retired in 2020 – probably to finally catch up on its favorite space soap operas.

QATAR

Middle East
population: 2,979,000
Size (sq miles): 4,468
Size (sq km): 11,571

A Country That's Growing Sea-Legs: Qatar is literally expanding, not by magic, but through land reclamation. They're building islands and extending their territory into the Persian Gulf. It's like Qatar decided to play real-life Minecraft and started creating new land patches.

The Falcon, A Feathery VIP: In Qatar, falcons are more than birds; they're like feathered VIPs. They even have their own passports to prevent smuggling. It's not unusual to see a falcon in first class on a Qatar Airways flight, probably enjoying better service than most of us ever will.

Doha's Skyline: Architectural Whimsy: The skyline of Doha, Qatar's capital, looks like it was designed by a group of imaginative kids with a futuristic Lego set. From the Torch Tower to the Sidra Medical and Research Center, the architecture in Doha is a blend of modern art and science fiction – a concrete manifestation of "the future is now."

REUNION ISLAND
France

Africa - Indian Ocean
population: 859,959
Size (sq miles): 970
Size (sq km): 2,511

Volcano Selfies, Anyone?: Piton de la Fournaise, one of the world's most active volcanoes, is Reunion's hot spot – literally. It's like the island has its own natural fireworks show. For thrill-seekers and Instagrammers alike, it's the ultimate backdrop. Just remember, it's hot lava, not hot coffee!

The Language Salad Bowl: In Reunion, they speak Réunion Creole, French, and a mix of other languages. It's like the island decided to throw a language party and everyone was invited. Here, saying 'hello' could be an adventure in linguistics!

A Melting Pot of Festivals: Reunion Island loves a good party, and with its mix of cultures, there's always something to celebrate. It's one of those rare places where every religion celebrates the festival of the others. From Indian Diwali to Chinese New Year, it's like the island is on a non-stop world tour of festivals. Every day is a potential party – no passport required!

ROMANIA

Eastern Europe
population: 19,127,774
Size (sq miles): 92,043
Size (sq km):   238,397

Home of Dracula's Castle: Romania is famous for Bran Castle, often linked to the Dracula legend. While the connection to Vlad the Impaler, the inspiration for Dracula, is tenuous, it doesn't stop tourists from flocking there. It's like Transylvania decided to capitalize on the vampire craze – fang-tastic for the local economy!

The Happy Cemetery: In the village of Săpânța, you'll find the Merry Cemetery. Each tombstone is brightly colored and adorned with a humorous poem about the deceased's life. It's like they believed in laughing in the face of death, literally. Probably the only cemetery where you'll leave with a smile!

A Land of Superlatives: The Parliament and the Transfagarasan: Romania is home to the world's second-largest administrative building, the Palace of the Parliament, second only to the Pentagon. Also, gear up for the Transfăgărășan road, dubbed by some as the most beautiful road in the world. It's like Romania is the friend who always has to have the bigger slice of pizza, but in this case, it's buildings and roads.

RUSSIA

Europe/Asia
population: 145,912,025
Size (sq miles): 6,601,668
Size (sq km): 17,098,242

The Russian Bath, aka Banya: The traditional Russian banya (bathhouse) isn't just about getting clean; it's a whole social event. You sweat, you chat, you hit each other with birch branches, and then jump into cold water. It's the ultimate Russian chill, literally and figuratively.

Nine Time Zones in One Country: Russia is so vast it covers nine time zones. You could have breakfast in one part of Russia and by lunchtime in another part, it's already tomorrow. Talk about time travel!

The Curious Case of Russian Dolls: Matryoshka dolls, the famous Russian nesting dolls, are a symbol of national craftsmanship. Each doll opens to reveal another smaller doll inside, and so on. It's the original surprise package, Russian style – each layer revealing a new little mystery.

RWANDA

Central Africa
population: 13,600,000
Size (sq miles): 10,169
Size (sq km): 26,338

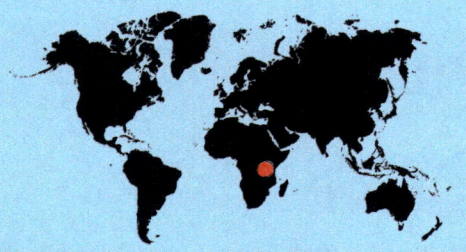

Land of a Thousand Hills: Rwanda is often called the 'Land of a Thousand Hills' due to its endless rolling hills. The country seems to have decided that flat is boring, and instead opted for a permanent roller-coaster landscape. Great for views, but maybe not so much for cycling!

Home to the Majestic Mountain Gorillas: One of the only places in the world to see mountain gorillas in the wild is Rwanda's Volcanoes National Park. These gorillas don't seem to mind the paparazzi and often grace visitors with what seems like a rehearsed show of raw, natural beauty and power.

The Cleanest Country in Africa: Rwanda takes cleanliness seriously. The last Saturday of each month is 'Umuganda', a national day of community cleaning. Everyone, including the President, gets their hands dirty (well, clean), making Rwanda probably the only country where you can end up picking litter next to the head of state.

SABA
The Netherlands

Carribbean
population: 1,537
Size (sq miles): 5
Size (sq km): 13

The Road That Couldn't Be Built: Saba's only road, aptly named "The Road," was built by locals after experts claimed it couldn't be done. The Sabans basically said, "Hold my beer," and now The Road is a winding masterpiece of stubborn determination and engineering.

Land of the Short Runway: Saba's Juancho E. Yrausquin Airport has the world's shortest commercial runway. Pilots landing here need nerves of steel and probably a good luck charm. It's the aviation equivalent of threading a needle while riding a unicycle.

Stairway to Heaven, Literally: The Mount Scenery hike in Saba features a stairway with over 1,000 steps leading to the island's highest point. It's the ultimate stairmaster challenge, but the breathtaking views at the top are a just reward. You'll feel on top of the world, if you can catch your breath!

SAINT KITTS AND NEVIS

Carribbean
population: 53,821
Size (sq miles): 104
Size (sq km): 269

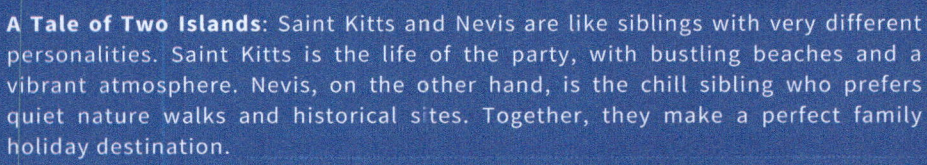

A Tale of Two Islands: Saint Kitts and Nevis are like siblings with very different personalities. Saint Kitts is the life of the party, with bustling beaches and a vibrant atmosphere. Nevis, on the other hand, is the chill sibling who prefers quiet nature walks and historical sites. Together, they make a perfect family holiday destination.

The Sugar Train: Once a sugar colony, Saint Kitts now has a scenic railway tour that takes you through old sugar plantations. It's a sweet ride, literally, offering stunning views and a glimpse into the island's sugary past. Just don't expect candy canes!

The Green Vervet Monkeys Outnumber Humans: Originally brought over by French settlers, the green vervet monkeys on Saint Kitts and Nevis have multiplied so much, they now outnumber humans! These mischievous primates are known for their love of 'borrowing' items from unsuspecting tourists. It's like living in a reverse zoo – here, the monkeys watch you!

SAINT LUCIA

Carribbean
population: 184,400
Size (sq miles): 238
Size (sq km): 617

The Pitons: Twin Peaks of Wonder: Saint Lucia is famous for the Pitons, two striking volcanic spires rising side by side from the sea. They're not just a stunning sight; they're also the island's best 'we're not in Kansas anymore' landmark. Hiking them is a rite of passage – like a stairway to heaven, but sweatier.

Drive-In Volcano, Anyone?: Ever wanted to drive into a volcano? The Sulphur Springs Park in Saint Lucia offers just that. It's the world's only drive-in volcano. Don't worry, it last erupted over 200 years ago, so the risk of a lava bath is pretty low.

Jump-Up Street Parties: Gros Islet, a town in Saint Lucia, hosts weekly 'Jump-Up' street parties. It's where locals and tourists alike groove to Caribbean beats, savor local food, and let their hair down. It's the island's way of saying, "Why wait for the weekend to have fun?"

SAINT VINCENT AND THE GRENADINES

Carribbean
population: 111,263
Size (sq miles): 150
Size (sq km):   389

Where Pirates Once Roamed: Saint Vincent and the Grenadines was one of the filming locations for the movie "Pirates of the Caribbean." The islands provided the perfect backdrop for swashbuckling adventures. Today, the only treasure hunters are tourists with cameras, looking for that perfect shot.

Vincy Mas - A Carnival of Color: The annual carnival, known as 'Vincy Mas,' is a vibrant explosion of music, dance, and color. It's the time when the islands come alive with calypso music, steel bands, and street parties. Think Mardi Gras, but with an unmistakable island twist.

The Breadfruit Saga: Breadfruit was introduced to the islands in the 18th century to provide cheap food for slaves. Today, it's a staple in the local cuisine. Whether roasted, fried, or made into chips, it's a carb lover's paradise. The islands might be the only place where being 'full of breadfruit' is a good thing!

SAMOA

Oceania
population: 200,874
Size (sq miles): 1,093
Size (sq km): 2,831

The Last Place to Say Goodbye to Today: Samoa is situated just west of the International Date Line. It was the last place on Earth to see the sunset each day until 2011, when it hopped across the line to be the first to see the sunrise. It's the closest you'll get to time travel in this day and age!

The Home of the Traditional Tattoo: Samoa is renowned for its traditional tattoos, or 'tatau', a practice with deep cultural significance. These aren't your typical walk-in studio tattoos. The Samoan tatau is a rite of passage, symbolizing courage and social status. It's an inked story of heritage, pain, and pride.

The To-Sua Ocean Trench: One of Samoa's natural wonders is the To-Sua Ocean Trench, a giant swimming hole connected to the ocean through an underwater cave. With lush gardens surrounding it, it's like nature dug out its own private pool, complete with a ladder. Just add water, and you have a tropical paradise!

SAN MARINO

Southern Europe
population: 34,232
Size (sq miles): 24
Size (sq km): 61

The Country That Climbed a Mountain: San Marino is built on top of Mount Titano. It's as if the country said, "Flat land? No, thanks. We prefer a panoramic view." The three towers atop its peaks have seen more history than most cities, and the view is a constant reminder that sometimes, the top is the best place to be.

Captains Regent: Double the Leadership: Instead of one president or prime minister, San Marino elects two Captains Regent every six months. It's teamwork taken to a national level. Imagine having two bosses at work, but they change before you learn how to spell their names.

A Haven for Car Enthusiasts: Despite its size, San Marino has a heart for fast cars. It hosts a Rally Legend event, attracting vintage and modern rally cars. For a few days a year, the quiet mountain roads transform into a haven for car enthusiasts. It's like the Monaco Grand Prix's charming little cousin, but with more hairpin turns and hill climbs.

SAO TOME AND PRINCIPE

Africa
population: 223,368
Size (sq miles): 372
Size (sq km):   964

Chocolate Paradise: Sao Tome and Principe is nicknamed the "Chocolate Islands," thanks to its rich, high-quality cocoa production. The islands are like a chocoholic's dream come true. Here, chocolate isn't just a treat; it's a way of life. Forget about Willy Wonka, this is the real deal!

The Bird Watchers' Bliss: These islands are a paradise for bird watchers, with more than 140 bird species, including some that are endemic. It's as if the birds hold their own exclusive parties, and only the most avid bird enthusiasts are invited. Binoculars are the ticket to this feathery fiesta!

A Coffee Lover's Dream: Coffee lovers, rejoice! Sao Tome and Principe produce some of the world's best Arabica coffee. The islands' volcanic soil and tropical climate create the perfect conditions for growing these beloved beans. It's like the islands decided to wake up and smell the coffee – and then decided to grow it, too.

SAUDI ARABIA

Middle East
population: 35,844,000
Size (sq miles): 830,000
Size (sq km): 2,149,690

The Empty Quarter: A Whole Lot of Sand: Rub' al Khali, also known as the Empty Quarter, is the largest contiguous sand desert in the world. It's so vast and empty, you could misplace an entire city in it and still have room for a beach resort. A perfect spot for those who really want to get away from it all – and then some.

Jeddah's Floating Mosque: In Jeddah, you'll find the Floating Mosque, which seems to hover over the Red Sea. At high tide, it looks like it's magically floating on water. A great place for prayer and pondering if you've suddenly developed water-walking abilities.

Coffee is King: In Saudi Arabia, serving coffee is an art and a sign of hospitality. It's not just about the caffeine; it's a social ritual. The traditional coffee, or 'qahwa', is flavored with cardamom and served in tiny cups. It's like saying, "Stay and chat awhile," but with more aroma and flavor.

SCOTLAND
United Kingdom

Western Europe
population: 5,466,000
Size (sq miles): 30,090
Size (sq km): 77,933

Land of Lochs and Legends: Scotland is famed for its lochs (lakes), with Loch Ness holding the crown, thanks to its elusive resident, Nessie, the Loch Ness Monster. Whether she's real or just playing the best game of hide-and-seek ever, she's certainly good for tourism.

Skirts for Men? Yes, Please!: The kilt, Scotland's traditional dress, is a skirt-like garment with a pattern (tartan) that represents different clans. It's a fashion statement and a history lesson all rolled into one. And let's be honest, who doesn't like a bit of breeze around their knees?

Haggis: The Chieftain of the Pudding Race: Haggis, Scotland's national dish, is a savory pudding containing sheep's heart, liver, and lungs, minced with onion, oatmeal, and spices. It's the kind of dish that sounds like a dare but ends up being surprisingly tasty. Or so the Scots say.

SENEGAL

West Africa
population: 17,196,301
Size (sq miles): 75,955
Size (sq km): 196,722

The Pink Lake: Lac Rose: Senegal is home to the remarkable Lake Retba, also known as Lac Rose (Pink Lake). It's famous for its striking pink color, caused by an algae. It's the perfect spot for those who thought regular lakes were just too mainstream and needed a splash of color.

The Door of No Return: The House of Slaves on Gorée Island, with its 'Door of No Return,' is a powerful monument to the Atlantic slave trade. It serves as a somber reminder of human cruelty and a symbol of hope and resilience. A visit here is a journey through the depths of human history.

Wrestling: In Senegal, wrestling, or 'Laamb', is not just a sport; it's a cultural phenomenon, blending athleticism with traditional rituals. Wrestlers train like Olympic athletes and are treated like rock stars. It's where sport meets tradition in a powerful display of strength and heritage.

SERBIA

Europe · Balkans
population: 6,926,705
Size (sq miles): 29,913
Size (sq km):   77,474

The Land of Superlative Raspberries: Serbia is one of the world's largest producers of raspberries, responsible for nearly a third of the global production. It's the berry heart of the world – if you love raspberries, you might as well call Serbia paradise.

A Clock Tower That's Always Late: In Belgrade, the Millennium Clock Tower is famously set to run several minutes late as a symbol of the laid-back lifestyle. It's the city's way of saying, "Relax, what's the hurry?" In Serbia, being a little late isn't wrong; it's just on time.

Exit Festival: Party in a Fortress: The Exit Festival, held in the Petrovaradin Fortress, is one of Europe's most renowned music festivals. It started as a student protest against the government and turned into an annual celebration of freedom and music. It's like history and partying came together and decided to throw a festival.

SEYCHELLES

Africa - Indian Ocean
population: 99,202
Size (sq miles): 176
Size (sq km): 455

Home of the Unique Coco de Mer: Seychelles is famous for the Coco de Mer, the world's largest nut, found only here. These nuts are so bizarrely shaped, they could be nature's own practical joke. Carrying one as a souvenir might require an extra suitcase, though!

The Aldabra, a Giant Tortoise Sanctuary: Aldabra Atoll in Seychelles is like a retirement home for giant tortoises, housing the world's largest population. These old-timers take life slow – really slow. Watching them is a reminder that sometimes the best pace is a leisurely one.

Beaches That Spoil You for Life: Seychelles boasts some of the most stunning beaches in the world, with powdery white sand and crystal-clear waters. After a visit here, other beaches might just seem... meh. It sets the beach bar sky-high – or should we say sea-deep?

SIERRA LEONE

West Africa
population: 8,141,343
Size (sq miles): 27,699
Size (sq km): 71,740

Freetown: Land of the Free: Freetown, the capital of Sierra Leone, was founded by freed slaves. Its very name speaks of liberty. This historical city isn't just about urban hustle; it's a living reminder that freedom is invaluable.

The Cotton Tree: A Living Monument: In the heart of Freetown stands an ancient cotton tree, a symbol of freedom for the slaves who settled the city. It's not just a tree; it's a natural monument to resilience and hope. Plus, it's probably the oldest living thing in the city that doesn't pay taxes.

A Paradise for Diverse Wildlife: Sierra Leone's Tiwai Island Wildlife Sanctuary is teeming with diverse wildlife, including eleven species of primates. It's like the island is hosting its own non-stop animal party, and humans are just the guests. A visit here is a crash course in primate behavior – minus the homework.

SINGAPORE

Southeast Asia
population: 5,453,600
Size (sq miles): 278
Size (sq km):   719

Chewing Gum Ban: In Singapore, selling chewing gum is banned. It's a place where minty fresh breath comes from mints, not gum. The streets are so clean, you could almost eat off them – but maybe stick to the amazing street food instead.

The SuperTree Grove: Gardens by the Bay features the futuristic SuperTree Grove, where giant tree-like structures tower over the gardens. By day, they provide shade; by night, they light up in a dazzling display. It's where nature meets sci-fi – the perfect backdrop for your next out-of-this-world selfie.

A Country of Foodies: Singapore is a paradise for food lovers, offering a melting pot of cuisines. The hawker centers are like food theme parks, where the rides are dishes from all over the world. Here, "Let's grab a bite" could lead to a culinary adventure spanning continents.

SLOVAKIA

Europe
population: 5,460,721
Size (sq miles): 18,933
Size (sq km): 49,035

Land of Castles: Slovakia might as well be nicknamed 'the land of castles'. Boasting over 100 castles and ruins, it's a paradise for history buffs and ghost hunters. Bratislava Castle, for instance, looks over the city like an old guardian, probably reminiscing about the good old medieval days.

More Caves Than a Batman Movie: With over 6,000 caves, Slovakia is a spelunker's dream come true. The most famous is the Dobšinská Ice Cave, a frozen wonderland all year round. It's nature's own ice museum - just don't expect any ice cream stands.

A Bridge Named After Chuck Norris?: In a 2012 poll, Slovaks almost named a new bridge after Chuck Norris. Yes, you read that right. The Chuck Norris Bridge. It shows the quirky sense of humor Slovaks have. In the end, they settled for a less roundhouse-kick-inspired name, but the legend lives on.

SLOVENIA

Europe
population: 2,102,678
Size (sq miles): 7,827
Size (sq km): 20,273

A Love Affair with Bees: Slovenia is big on beekeeping. It's not just a hobby; it's almost a national sport. They even have painted beehive panels, turning apiaries into art galleries. In Slovenia, a bee isn't just a bee; it's a tiny, buzzing national treasure.

The Human Fish in Underground Caves: Slovenia's Postojna Cave is home to the olm, also known as the 'human fish' due to its skin color. These little cave-dwellers can live up to 100 years and are practically blind. It's like they decided evolution was overrated and opted for a simple, dark, and serene cave life.

The Short but Sweet Coastline: Slovenia has just 46.6 km of coastline, but it's packed with charm. The coastal town of Piran is like a slice of Venice, minus the crowds and gondolas. It proves the saying, "Good things come in small packages," especially when that package includes a gorgeous Adriatic beach.

SOLOMON ISLANDS

Oceania
population: 703,996
Size (sq miles): 11,157
Size (sq km): 28,896

A Nation of Islands: The Solomon Islands are made up of nearly 1,000 islands. It's a place where you can literally island-hop until you drop. With so many islands, choosing your favorite is like trying to pick a favorite chocolate in a mega assorted box – impossible but delightful.

The Underwater Museum: The waters around the Solomon Islands are a graveyard of WWII shipwrecks and planes. These historical remnants have become an underwater museum, attracting divers from all over the world. It's history meets adventure – with a side of coral.

The Talking Drums: In the Solomon Islands, traditional communication was done using 'talking drums'. These drums could send complex messages across long distances, long before the days of texting. It's like ancient WhatsApp, but with more rhythm and no blue ticks.

SOMALIA

East Africa
population: 16,359,504
Size (sq miles): 246,201
Size (sq km): 637,657

The Land of Poets: Somalia is often called the "Nation of Poets." Here, poetry is a cherished form of expression, so much so that political debates and love letters have been done in verse. It's where words weave magic, and a good rhyme might just be more powerful than a sword.

Camel Country: Somalia has more camels than any other country in the world. These aren't just animals; they're a symbol of wealth and status. A Somali proverb goes, "A man without a camel is like a man without a life." It's the ultimate camel paradise, minus the humps.

The Historic Laas Geel Caves: The Laas Geel caves, hidden away in the Somali desert, house some of the oldest cave paintings in Africa, dating back around 5,000 years. They're like ancient graffiti, showcasing early man's love for art. It's a prehistoric art gallery, and admission is free!

SOUTH AFRICA

Southern Africa
population: 60,756,135
Size (sq miles): 470,693
Size (sq km):   1,219,090

Table Mountain: A Flat-Topped Wonder: Table Mountain in Cape Town is famous for its flat top, which often sports a "tablecloth" of clouds. It's as if nature said, "Let's make a mountain that doubles as a dining table for giants."

The Cradle of Humankind: The Cradle of Humankind, a World Heritage site near Johannesburg, is where some of the world's oldest hominid fossils have been found. It's humanity's ancestral home, sort of like visiting your great-great-great (add a few thousand more 'greats') grandparents' house.

The Great Braai Tradition: In South Africa, a 'braai' (barbecue) is not just a way to cook food; it's a social event, a national pastime, and practically a religion. It's where you'll find South Africans bonding over fire, meat, and storytelling. The unofficial motto? "If it can be cooked, it can be braaied."

SOUTH KOREA

East Asia
population: 51,709,098
Size (sq miles): 38,750
Size (sq km): 100,363

Cafe Culture to the Extreme: South Korea takes its cafe culture seriously. You'll find cafes in every theme imaginable, from animal cafes to ones where you can enjoy a latte in a replica of a European village. It's a caffeine lover's dream, where your biggest decision might be, "Do I sip my coffee with cats, dogs, or surrounded by pink flamingos today?"

The Digital Detox Capsules: In a country known for its tech-savvy population, South Korea offers 'digital detox' programs in prison-like facilities. It's a voluntary escape for those who need a break from screens. Think of it as a tech timeout, but you're the one behind bars.

Love for Fermented Cabbage: Kimchi, the staple side dish in South Korea, is more than just fermented cabbage. It's a national obsession, a source of pride, and there are hundreds of varieties. Each family has their own recipe, and yes, it's a big deal – a sort of culinary heritage passed down through generations.

SOUTH SUDAN

Africa
population: 11,381,378
Size (sq miles): 239,285
Size (sq km): 619,745

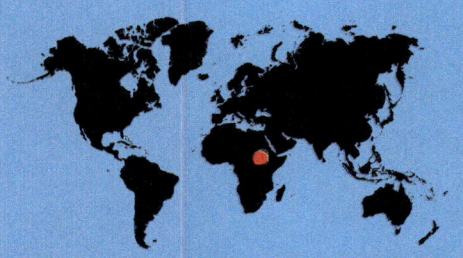

The World's Newest Country: South Sudan is the world's newest country, gaining independence in 2011. It's like the world's youngest sibling, still figuring out its place at the global dinner table. Here, history isn't just in the past; it's being made every day.

A Multitude of Languages: In South Sudan, over 60 different languages are spoken. It's a linguistic jigsaw puzzle, with each piece representing a different community and culture. Conversations here can be a real-life game of language bingo.

Wrestling as a National Sport: Wrestling is more than a sport in South Sudan; it's a cultural spectacle. Wrestlers are local heroes, and matches are vibrant events with dancing, music, and colorful attire. It's like a combination of a sports match and a festival, where strength and tradition wrestle hand in hand.

SPAIN

Southern Europe
population: 47,351,567
Size (sq miles): 195,364
Size (sq km):   505,992

The Sun-Soaked Coastline: Spain has over 5,000 miles of coastline, which basically means endless beaches. If Spain were a person at a party, it would be the one with the best tan, telling stories about sunny days and siestas.

The Sagrada Família: Forever a Work in Progress: Barcelona's Sagrada Família has been under construction for over 130 years. It's the architectural equivalent of "I'll be ready in five minutes" turning into a few hours. This basilica is proof that in Spain, patience isn't just a virtue; it's a way of life.

The Siesta: A National Institution: Spain runs on its own schedule. People eat lunch at 2pm and dine at 10, and the siesta is a cherished tradition. It's a time, from 2 to 6 pm when shops close, and streets empty, as people take a mid-afternoon break. This practice is less about laziness and more about making time to enjoy life – or just to avoid the midday heat. Either way, it's a custom many wish they could export!

SRI LANKA

South Asia
population: 21,803,000
Size (sq miles): 25,332
Size (sq km): 65,610

Eight World Heritage Sites in a Tiny Island: Sri Lanka may be small, but it's packed with a whopping eight UNESCO World Heritage Sites. From ancient cities to dense forests, it's as if the island is showing off its historical and natural beauty in a grand global exhibition.

The Stilt Fishermen of Galle: In Galle, fishermen take to stilts for their catch. Perched on narrow poles in the shallow waters, they fish with a skill that's part balance, part patience. It's fishing taken to acrobatic heights, literally!

The Land of Cinnamon and Tea: Sri Lanka is known as the land where the best cinnamon and some of the finest tea in the world come from. It's like the island is hosting an eternal tea party, and cinnamon is the guest of honor. Teatime here could well be a fragrant journey through lush fields and aromatic spice gardens.

ST EUSTATIUS
The Netherlands

Carribbean
population: 3,138
Size (sq miles): 8
Size (sq km): 21

The Historical "First Salute": St Eustatius, a tiny island in the Caribbean, played a big role in American history. It was the first foreign entity to officially recognize the United States' independence by saluting an American warship in 1776. This small island made a grand gesture, essentially high-fiving America in its fight for independence.

Sleeping with a Volcano: The island is dominated by a dormant volcano named The Quill. It's not every day you get to say, "I live next to a sleeping giant." For the adventurous, hiking The Quill is like a journey to the center of the earth, only without the scary dinosaurs.

Diving into Riches: St Eustatius is a diver's paradise with shipwrecks scattered around its waters, remnants of its days as a trading hub. Exploring these underwater time capsules is like swimming through a history lesson, but with more fish and fewer textbooks.

ST MARTEEN

The Netherlands / France

Carribbean
population: 42,876
Size (sq miles): 13
Size (sq km):   34

A Tale of Two Nations: St. Maarten/St. Martin is unique as it's split between two countries: France and the Netherlands. It's like the island couldn't decide which European country it liked best, so it chose both. Crossing from one side to the other, you can have a croissant for breakfast and a stroopwafel for dessert!

Airport Beach Thrills: Maho Beach is famous for its proximity to the airport, where planes fly incredibly low to land. It's the perfect spot for thrill-seekers and aviation enthusiasts who like their beach days with a side of jet engines.

The Smallest Landmass Shared by Two Nations: At just 37 square miles, this island is the world's smallest landmass shared by two countries. It's a cozy arrangement, where the Dutch side is known for its lively party atmosphere and the French side for its tranquil beaches. It's like having a party house and a chill zone all in one.

SUDAN

Africa
population: 45,561,556
Size (sq miles): 718,723
Size (sq km):   1,861,484

More Pyramids than Egypt: Sudan is home to more pyramids than Egypt, boasting over 200 of these ancient wonders. It's as if Sudan quietly said, "Hold my beer" while everyone was busy staring at Giza. These lesser-known pyramids offer a glimpse into a rich, ancient history without the bustling crowds.

The Whirling Dervishes of Omdurman: Every Friday in Omdurman, you can witness the mesmerizing dance of the Whirling Dervishes. It's a spiritual performance where dancers spin in rhythmic circles, wearing colorful robes. It's part dance, part prayer, and wholly captivating.

A Country of Contrasts: Sudan features a remarkable geographical diversity. From the sprawling Sahara Desert to the lush regions along the Nile, it's a land of stark contrasts. In one day, you could be sweating in the vast desert and then sipping tea on the banks of the Nile, watching life flow by.

SURINAME

South America
population: 630,000
Size (sq miles): 63,251
Size (sq km):   163,820

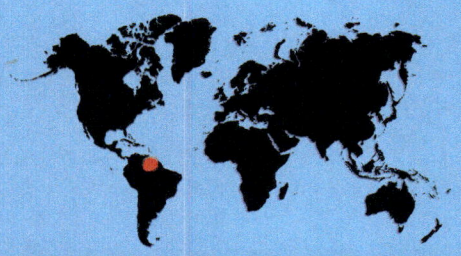

Land of Water: Suriname is dominated by rivers, with the Suriname River running like a main highway through the country. It's the go-to place for a swim, a boat ride, or just to wave at the passing fish. It's as if the country decided roads were too mainstream and rivers were the way to go.

A Melting Pot of Languages: With Dutch as the official language and a mix of other languages like Sranan Tongo, Hindi, and Javanese, Suriname is a linguistic cocktail. It's the kind of place where a conversation can switch languages mid-sentence and nobody bats an eye.

The Saint Peter and Paul Cathedral: Suriname's capital, Paramaribo, is home to one of the largest wooden buildings in the Western Hemisphere - the Saint Peter and Paul Cathedral. This cathedral is like the architectural equivalent of a giant, holy treehouse. It's a towering reminder that sometimes, the best art is carved, not painted.

SWEDEN

Northern Europe · Scandinavia
population: 10,379,295
Size (sq miles): 173,860
Size (sq km):   450,295

Midsummer Madness: Sweden takes midsummer celebrations to another level. It's when Swedes dance around a maypole, resembling a flower-crowned conga line. This festival is a serious business – it's about joy, light, and convincing your friends to dance like frogs. Yes, frogs.

The Northern Lights Hideout: In the Swedish Lapland, you can witness the mesmerizing Northern Lights. It's nature's own light show, where the sky decides to throw a disco for the stars. And the best part? No entrance fee.

Fika – More Than a Coffee Break: 'Fika' is a concept in Sweden, a coffee break but with a focus on socializing. It involves coffee, sweet treats, and friends. In Sweden, fika is essential; it's like a national sport but with more pastries and less sweating.

SWITZERLAND

Europe
population: 8,700,000
Size (sq miles): 15,940
Size (sq km): 41,290

Four Languages, One Country: Switzerland is a linguistic smorgasbord with four official languages: German, French, Italian, and Romansh. It's a country where saying "hello" can turn into a mini United Nations conference.

A Haven for Cuckoo Clocks (Not Really): Contrary to popular belief, cuckoo clocks originate from Germany, not Switzerland. But the Swiss won't mind if you think otherwise. They're too busy making delicious chocolate and precise watches to correct you every time.

The Land of Lakes and Mountains: With over 1,500 lakes, Switzerland has enough water to make a fish consider a career in real estate. And let's not forget the Alps, which cover a good 60% of the country's land area. In Switzerland, you're either going up a mountain or down to a lake – it's nature's ultimate workout plan.

SYRIA

Middle East
population: 18,275,702
Size (sq miles): 71,498
Size (sq km):   185,180

The Ancient City of Aleppo: Aleppo, one of the oldest continuously inhabited cities in the world, has seen more history than most textbooks. It's a city where every stone and corner has a story, some dating back to the 6th millennium BCE. It's like a living museum, except the exhibits need a bit of restoration work.

The Souk of All Souks: The Al-Hamidiyah Souk in Damascus is not just any market; it's a bazaar out of a storybook. With its narrow alleys and the sunlight streaming through the metal roof, shopping here is like a treasure hunt, minus the map and the pirates.

A Sweet Tooth for Baklava: Syrian baklava isn't just a dessert; it's a national treasure. Layers of phyllo pastry, nuts, and syrup come together in a sweet symphony. It's like the culinary version of a hug – warm, comforting, and always welcome.

TAIWAN

East Asia
population: 23,855,000
Size (sq miles): 13,974
Size (sq km): 36,193

Bubble Tea Bonanza: Taiwan is the birthplace of bubble tea, a national obsession that has bubbled over into a global phenomenon. It's a drink, a snack, and a way to challenge your multitasking skills – all in one cup.

The Tower with a Twist: The Taipei 101 tower, once the world's tallest building, is designed to withstand typhoons and earthquakes. It's like Mother Nature met her match in a skyscraper. Plus, it has one of the world's fastest elevators – it's practically a ride in an amusement park.

A Lantern Festival Like No Other: The Pingxi Lantern Festival lights up the sky with thousands of paper lanterns, each carrying wishes and dreams into the night. It's a spectacle of hope and beauty, turning the sky into a canvas of twinkling lights. It's like sending a text message to the universe.

TAJIKISTAN

Central Asia
population: 9,749,627
Size (sq miles): 55,251
Size (sq km):   143,100

The Roof of the World: Over 90% of Tajikistan is mountainous, earning it the nickname "The Roof of the World." It's the perfect destination for anyone who thinks flat landscapes are just too mainstream and prefers their scenery with a bit of altitude.

The Pamir Highway: The Pamir Highway, one of the highest roads in the world, offers a road trip like no other. It's where you drive above the clouds, and the journey feels as epic as the destination. Just don't forget to pack your sense of adventure along with some extra oxygen!

The Strangest National Sport (ever): Buzkashi, the national sport, is like polo, but with a goat carcass instead of a ball. It's a test of strength, horsemanship, and, well, one's ability to handle a goat. Definitely not a sport for the faint-hearted or those easily spooked by farm animals.

TANZANIA

East Africa
population: 61,741,120
Size (sq miles): 365,755
Size (sq km):   947,303

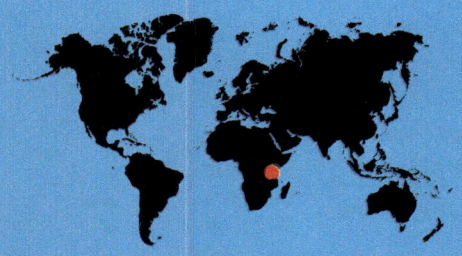

The Serengeti's Great Migration: The Serengeti National Park in Tanzania is famous for the Great Migration, where millions of wildebeest and zebras make an epic journey in search of greener pastures. It's the animal kingdom's version of a road trip, but with more drama and a lot more hooves.

The Snows of Kilimanjaro: Mount Kilimanjaro, Africa's highest peak, is right here in Tanzania. It's one of the few places on the equator where you can find snow. It's as if Kilimanjaro wanted to stand out and chose a snowy cap to do so. A true fashionista of the mountain world!

Zanzibar's Stone Town: Stone Town in Zanzibar is a cultural melting pot with a labyrinth of narrow streets. It's a place where history whispers from every corner and building. Walking through Stone Town is like strolling through a live museum, except the exhibits are actual people going about their daily lives.

THAILAND

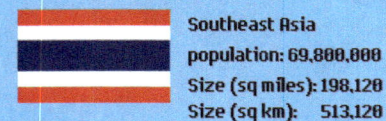

Southeast Asia
population: 69,800,000
Size (sq miles): 198,120
Size (sq km):   513,120

The Land of Smiles: Thailand is often called the "Land of Smiles." Smiling is an integral part of Thai culture, symbolizing friendliness and warmth. It's a place where you can receive a smile for just about anything – whether you're buying a mango, asking for directions, or even when you're lost in translation.

Water Fight Festival: The Songkran Festival, marking the Thai New Year, is essentially the world's largest water fight. For three days, the entire country engages in a good-natured water battle, armed with water guns, buckets, and hoses. It's a time when being soaked from head to toe means good luck, and nobody is too old to play.

A Haven for Street Food: Thailand's street food is legendary. Every corner seems to offer a culinary adventure, from spicy Pad Thai to sweet mango sticky rice. It's a never-ending buffet, where every meal is a journey through taste and aroma. The Thai street food scene is like an open-air, all-you-can-eat restaurant, minus the walls and the waiter.

TIBET
China

Asia
population: 3,500,000
Size (sq miles): 471,700
Size (sq km): 1,221,600

The Roof of the World: Tibet is often referred to as the "Roof of the World" because of its towering Himalayan peaks. It's so high up that if you're not careful, you might bump your head on the sky. It's the ultimate destination for anyone who literally wants to be on top of the world.

Butter Tea, Anyone?: In Tibet, butter tea is a staple. It's a unique blend of tea, yak butter, and salt. Think of it as the Tibetan version of a morning latte – only butterier, saltier, and probably an acquired taste for anyone who's not a yak.

The Potala Palace: A Fortress in the Clouds: The Potala Palace in Lhasa, the historic home of the Dalai Lama, is an architectural wonder perched high on a hill. This massive structure, with over a thousand rooms, is like a maze of spirituality and history, offering views that literally take your breath away – partly because of the altitude.

TIMOR-LESTE

Oceania
population: 1,300,000
Size (sq miles): 5,760
Size (sq km):   14,919

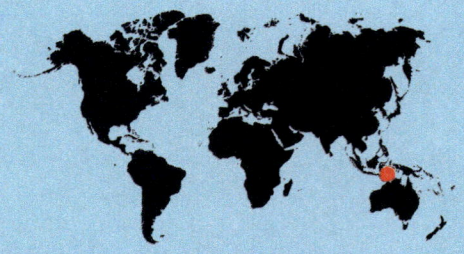

A Nation Born in the New Millennium: Timor-Leste, or East Timor, is one of the world's youngest countries, gaining independence in 2002. It's the adolescent of nations, still finding its feet but full of potential and ready to make its mark on the world stage.

Coffee with a Cause: Timor-Leste is renowned for its organic coffee, a major source of income for many locals. These coffee beans don't just wake you up; they help keep a nation's economy buzzing. It's like your morning brew is helping to fuel a whole country.

The Legend of the Crocodile: A popular Timorese legend says the island was formed from a crocodile. The story goes that a small crocodile transformed into the island as a reward for a boy's kindness. Today, the island's shape resembles a crocodile, and the creature is revered. It's like a fairytale come to life, except here, the crocodile is the hero.

TOGO

Africa
population: 8,300,000
Size (sq miles): 21,925
Size (sq km): 56,785

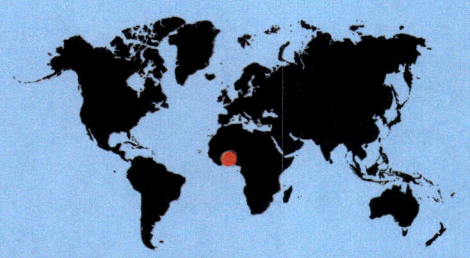

The Smiley Coastline: Togo might have one of the shortest coastlines in Africa, just 56 km, but it's packed with smiles and sunshine. The coastline is like a cheerful welcome mat, inviting you to enjoy its sandy beaches and vibrant markets.

Fetish Markets: A Different Kind of Shopping: Lomé, the capital, is home to one of the world's largest fetish (voodoo) markets. Here, you can find anything from animal skulls to traditional medicines. It's like a supermarket for the supernatural, where every item has a story more intriguing than the last.

The Land of Stilt Villages: In Togo, you can visit stilt villages in Lake Togo, where entire communities live above water. These villages aren't just surviving; they're thriving. It's like Venice, but with a West African twist – more fishing canoes, less gondolas.

TOKELAU

Oceania
population: 1,500
Size (sq miles): 4
Size (sq km): 10

Solar-Powered Life: Tokelau is the first country to run entirely on solar power. It's as if the sun looked at Tokelau and said, "You guys need a hand?" and Tokelau replied, "Yes, please!" Now, this tiny island nation basks not just in sunshine, but also in its eco-friendly achievements.

A Nation of Water Villages: With no airports, reaching Tokelau is a feat of its own, typically involving a long boat ride. The atolls are so remote, they're like secret hideouts, perfect for anyone who's ever wanted to escape the hustle and bustle of big city life.

The Coconut Wireless: In the absence of widespread internet or telephones, Tokelauans rely on a more personal network of communication, often jokingly referred to as the 'coconut wireless'. It's the original social media – island style – where news travels as fast as a stroll on the beach.

TONGA

Oceania
population: 100,000
Size (sq miles): 290
Size (sq km): 750

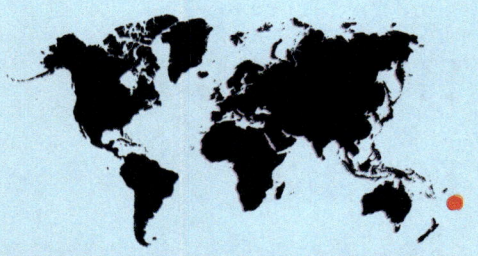

The Only Independent Kingdom in the Pacific: Tonga holds the title of being the only remaining monarchy in the Pacific. It's a kingdom where the royal family isn't just a ceremonial relic but a part of everyday life. Think less 'The Crown' and more 'Island Royalty'.

Flying Foxes as Sacred Creatures: In Tonga, flying foxes (fruit bats) are considered sacred and are protected by royal decree. They're like the royal guards of the animal kingdom, only less about guarding and more about hanging upside down from trees.

An Underwater Volcanic Show: Tonga sits on the Pacific Ring of Fire, leading to some spectacular underwater volcanic activity. It's as if Mother Nature is putting on a fireworks display, but underwater and with more lava. A true spectacle for adventurous divers!

TRINIDAD AND TOBAGO

Carribbean
population: 1,400,000
Size (sq miles): 1,980
Size (sq km):   5,130

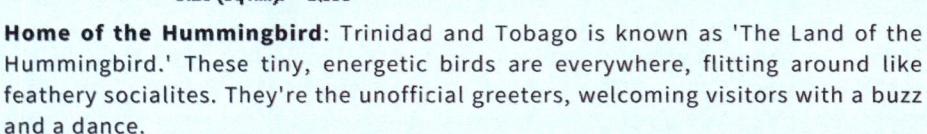

Home of the Hummingbird: Trinidad and Tobago is known as 'The Land of the Hummingbird.' These tiny, energetic birds are everywhere, flitting around like feathery socialites. They're the unofficial greeters, welcoming visitors with a buzz and a dance.

The Birthplace of Steelpan: This twin-island nation gave the world the steelpan, the only acoustic musical instrument invented in the 20th century. It's the soundtrack of the islands, turning every event into a potential steelpan jam session.

A Carnival of Colors: Trinidad's Carnival is one of the world's greatest street parties, bursting with vibrant costumes, calypso music, and non-stop dancing. It's where the whole country turns into a dance floor, and life is a parade. Literally!

TUNISIA

North Africa
population: 11,700,000
Size (sq miles): 63,170
Size (sq km):   163,610

The Real-Life Tatooine: Fans of Star Wars might recognize Tunisia as the filming location for Tatooine, Luke Skywalker's home planet. The original sets are still there, slowly being reclaimed by the desert. It's the perfect destination for those who've ever wanted to live out their intergalactic fantasies, minus the space travel.

A History Written in Mosaics: Tunisia is famous for its ancient Roman mosaics, a testament to its rich history. These aren't just old tiles; they're like storybooks made of stone, telling tales from centuries past. Visiting the Bardo Museum in Tunis is like stepping into an art gallery where every piece tells a historical tale.

The Festival of the Camel: The Festival of the Sahara in Douz is a celebration of desert life, featuring camel racing, dancing, and Bedouin music. It's like the Burning Man of the desert, but with more camels and fewer art cars. This festival is a cultural deep dive into the heart of the Tunisian desert.

TURKEY

Europe/Asia
population: 84,300,000
Size (sq miles): 302,535
Size (sq km):   783,562

Two Continents, One Country: Turkey is a land straddling two continents, Europe and Asia, separated by the bustling Bosphorus Strait. It's a place where you can have breakfast in Europe and lunch in Asia without ever leaving the city. Istanbul is like a bridge with a split personality – in the best possible way.

The Underground Cities of Cappadocia: Beneath the lunar-like landscape of Cappadocia lie entire underground cities, like Kaymaklı and Derinkuyu. These were ancient hideouts, not for outlaws, but for entire communities. Exploring them is like playing real-life Minecraft, only with more history and fewer pixelated monsters.

Turkish Delights and Bazaars: Turkish cuisine is a feast for the senses, especially the sweets. Turkish Delight, or lokum, isn't just a treat; it's a sugary symbol of hospitality. And let's not forget the Grand Bazaar in Istanbul – a shopping maze where you can haggle for anything from spices to silk. It's like stepping into Aladdin's cave, only with more bargaining and less magic carpet.

TURKMENISTAN

Central Asia
population: 6,000,000
Size (sq miles): 188,456
Size (sq km): 488,100

The Door to Hell: The Darvaza Gas Crater, known as the 'Door to Hell', is a fiery pit in the Karakum Desert that's been burning for decades. It's like nature's own barbecue pit, except you wouldn't want to cook your marshmallows over it. A surreal sight, especially at night, it's literally a hot tourist spot.

A Love for White Marble: Ashgabat, the capital of Turkmenistan, holds the world record for having the most white marble-clad buildings. It's as if the city was playing a game of dress-up and white marble was the only costume choice. On a sunny day, it's like walking inside a giant pearl.

The King of Melons: Turkmenistan takes its melons seriously, even celebrating an annual Melon Day. These aren't just any melons; they're sweet, juicy, and a matter of national pride. It's like having a day dedicated to celebrating your favorite fruit, but with parades, music, and more melons than you could imagine.

TURKS AND CAICOS

United Kingdom

Carribbean
population: 38,000
Size (sq miles): 238
Size (sq km):   616

The Conch Haven: Turks and Caicos is famous for its conch shells. These aren't just pretty seaside souvenirs; they're a culinary staple. It's a place where you can hear the ocean in a shell and then have it for lunch.

A Magnet for Humpback Whales: Every year, the islands become a gathering spot for humpback whales migrating to warmer waters. It's like the whales chose Turks and Caicos for their winter vacation – who can blame them?

The Underwater Drop-Off: The islands are home to one of the most impressive coral reefs and a dramatic underwater wall at Grand Turk. Diving here is like stepping off the edge of the world, but with more fish and less existential dread.

TUVALU

Oceania
population: 11,000
Size (sq miles): 10
Size (sq km): 26

An Internet Domain Powerhouse: Oddly enough, Tuvalu's internet domain '.tv' is a major source of income. It's popular with television channels and streaming platforms. This tiny island nation basically rents out virtual real estate to the world's media giants.

Rising Tides, Sinking Fears: As one of the lowest-lying countries in the world, Tuvalu is on the front lines of climate change. It's a nation with a water view in every direction, just more than they would like. The rising sea levels have them campaigning for global environmental awareness – and maybe looking for some tall friends.

A Nation Without Rivers: Tuvalu is one of the few countries in the world without any rivers. It's all about the ocean here. Why have rivers when you can have the vast Pacific? It's like choosing a whole cake instead of a slice.

UGANDA

East Africa
population: 45,700,000
Size (sq miles): 93,065
Size (sq km): 241,038

The Source of the Nile: Uganda is home to the source of the Nile River. It's like having the start button of one of the world's longest rivers. Here, you can literally stand at the birthplace of the Nile and ponder over where all that water is headed.

Banana Bonanza: Ugandans love their bananas, and not just the sweet kind. They have over 50 different varieties, including the green cooking banana, or matoke, a national dish. In Uganda, a meal without a banana is like a day without sunshine.

Gorilla Haven: The Bwindi Impenetrable National Park in Uganda is one of the last refuges for the endangered mountain gorilla. It's an exclusive club, and the gorillas are the VIP members. Trekking through the park is like a real-life game of 'Where's Waldo?' but with gorillas in a vast green forest.

UKRAINE

Eastern Europe
population: 41,000,000
Size (sq miles): 233,062
Size (sq km): 603,628

A Country with a Heart in its Geography: Ukraine's geographical center is near the small town of Rakhiv, aptly dubbed the "Heart of Europe." It's as if Ukraine is Europe's beating heart, albeit one surrounded by picturesque mountains rather than arteries.

The Tunnel of Love: In Klevan, there's a verdant green tunnel known as the "Tunnel of Love." It's a favorite spot for couples, where a train path has turned into a romantic, leafy corridor. It's nature and romance teaming up to create the perfect backdrop for those dreamy Instagram posts.

Chicken Kyiv: A Delicious Misnomer: Contrary to popular belief, Chicken Kyiv (or Kiev) might not have originated in Ukraine's capital city. But that doesn't stop locals and visitors from enjoying this delectable dish of breaded chicken with a buttery core. Who cares about the name, anyway.

ABU DHABI
United Arab Emirates

Middle East
population: 9,800,000
Size (sq miles): 32,300
Size (sq km):   83,600

The Leaning Tower of Abu Dhabi: The Capital Gate building in Abu Dhabi holds the world record for the world's farthest leaning man-made tower. It leans more than the Leaning Tower of Pisa, but without the same risk of toppling over. It's like the tower decided to do a bit of a stretch and just stayed that way.

A Desert Rose City: Abu Dhabi's Al Ain, also known as the Garden City, is a stark contrast to the surrounding desert, blooming with greenery and life. It's like an oasis that decided to go big, proving that even in the desert, you can have a green thumb.

Falconry: A Sport of Kings and Sheikhs: In Abu Dhabi, falconry is more than a sport; it's a revered cultural tradition. Falcons can even get their own passports for travel. It's a place where your bird of prey is almost as important as your smartphone – great for selfies, but with more feathers.

DUBAI
United Arab Emirates

Middle East
population: 9,800,000
Size (sq miles): 32,300
Size (sq km):   83,600

A City That Loves to Break Records: Dubai is a city of superlatives. Home to the world's tallest building, the Burj Khalifa, it's like Dubai is constantly saying, "Go big or go home." The city loves breaking records so much, you half expect the next world's biggest something to be announced during your visit.

The Indoor Ski Resort: In the middle of the desert, Dubai boasts an indoor ski resort, Ski Dubai. It's as if the city looked at the scorching sun and said, "Nice try, but we want snow." Perfect for those who love winter sports but aren't big fans of actual winter, though it may not be the most planet friendly activity.

The Gold ATM: Dubai even has ATMs that dispense gold bars. It's like regular ATMs felt too mundane, so they added a Midas touch. If withdrawing cash feels too ordinary, why not a 24-karat gold souvenir?

UNITED STATES

North America
population: 331,000,000
Size (sq miles): 3,796,742
Size (sq km):   9,833,520

Gigantic Green Lady: Ever heard of a massive green lady holding a torch? That's the Statue of Liberty in New York! She's not just a giant fashion model; she represents freedom and was a gift from France in 1886. Imagine getting a birthday present that's 151 feet tall and having to find a place to keep it!

Land of Super-Sized Meals: In the USA, everything's bigger, especially the food portions. A regular meal might look like it's made for a giant. If you order a small drink, don't be surprised if it's the size of a bucket!

The Great Melting Pot: America is like a giant mixing bowl of cultures. People from all around the world live here, bringing their traditions, foods, and languages. So, you might hear Spanish, Chinese, and even Hindi while walking down a street. And for dinner? You could have Italian pizza, Mexican tacos, and Chinese fortune cookies all in one meal!

240

URUGUAY

South America
population: 3,500,000
Size (sq miles): 68,037
Size (sq km): 176,215

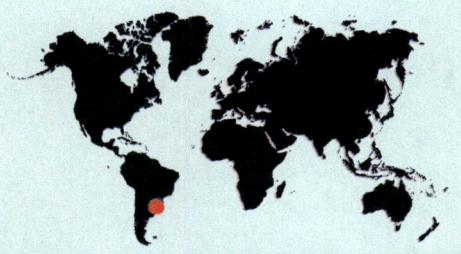

Cows Outnumber People: In Uruguay, cows seem to have taken over. There are more cows than people! Imagine going to school and realizing there are more cows chilling in the fields than classmates in the playground. Maybe cows enjoy the lovely Uruguay scenery too!

Soccer Fever Everywhere: Uruguayans are crazy about soccer – or football, as they call it. It's not just a game; it's like a national holiday every time there's a match. Even the cows probably pause to watch the game. And remember, Uruguay hosted the first ever World Cup in 1930, which they won!

Mate Mania: If you're thirsty in Uruguay, forget soda – it's all about Mate (pronounced mah-tey). This traditional drink, sipped from a shared cup, is a big deal. It's like a social network but in a drink form. People gather, share stories, and pass the Mate around. It's friend-request, Uruguay style!

US VIRGIN ISLANDS

United States

Carribbean
population: 104,000
Size (sq miles): 133
Size (sq km): 346

Drive on the Left, American Style: In the US Virgin Islands, they drive on the left side of the road, which is quite unusual for an American territory. It's like they decided to mix British driving rules with American cars – most of which are left-hand drives!

The Island of Pirates: Once a hotspot for pirates, the US Virgin Islands have a rich history of swashbuckling tales. Legend says that famous pirates like Blackbeard used to hang out here. So, if you're searching for treasure, you might just be in the right place – just don't forget your pirate hat!

A Carnival That Lasts a Month: Love parties? The US Virgin Islands celebrate Carnival for an entire month! It's a festival of colors, music, dancing, and food. Imagine having a birthday party that lasts for weeks instead of just a day. Now that's how you throw a party, island style!

UZBEKISTAN

Central Asia
population: 33,900,000
Size (sq miles): 172,742
Size (sq km): 447,400

City of Blue Domes: Samarkand, a city in Uzbekistan, is known for its stunning blue domes. They're not just blue; they're like the sky decided to settle on buildings! You can't play hide and seek here because the domes are so bright and visible, you'd be found in no time.

Bread That's a Work of Art: Uzbek bread, called "non", isn't just tasty, it's also a masterpiece. Each loaf is decorated with unique patterns, made by pressing fingers into the dough – like edible fingerprint art. Forget sandwiches, you might just want to frame this bread on your wall!

Wedding Capes for Men: In Uzbekistan, grooms wear a special cape called a "chapan" at weddings. It's not just any cape – it's like a superhero's, but with traditional designs. So, if you attend an Uzbek wedding, don't be surprised to see a groom looking like he's about to save the world, right after cutting the cake.

VANUATU

Oceania
population: 307,000
Size (sq miles): 4,706
Size (sq km): 12,189

Land of Many Languages: Vanuatu is the place to be if you love languages. With over 100 languages spoken across its islands, it's like a giant language buffet! You could say "hello" in a different language every day for three months and still have some to spare.

The Original Bungee Jumpers: Forget bungee cords; in Vanuatu, they use vines! The people of Pentecost Island invented land diving, leaping off tall wooden towers with vines tied to their ankles. It's their way of proving their bravery and ensuring a good yam harvest. So, if you think your school's high dive is scary, think again!

The Happiest Place on Earth?: Vanuatu often ranks as one of the happiest places in the world. Maybe it's the beautiful beaches, the friendly people, or perhaps it's just because they have so many holidays. Seriously, they have more public holidays than almost any other country. It's like there's always a party waiting to happen!

VATICAN CITY

Southern Europe
population: 800
Size (sq miles): 0.17
Size (sq km):   0.44

Tiny but Mighty: Vatican City is the world's smallest independent state, so small that you could jog around its entire border during a lunch break. It's like having a whole country in the space of a shopping mall – complete with its own post office and radio station!

A Pope Mobile, Not a Batmobile: The Pope doesn't have a Batmobile, but he does have a Pope Mobile! It's a special vehicle designed to keep him safe while he greets crowds. Think of it as a mix between a car and a fishbowl on wheels. Definitely a unique ride!

Chimney Signals: When a new Pope is chosen, the news is announced through smoke signals from a chimney in the Sistine Chapel. White smoke means "we have a Pope!" and black smoke means "try again tomorrow." It's like ancient texting, but with smoke. Next time you see a chimney, just imagine it's sending you a message!

VENEZUELA

South America
population: 28,500,000
Size (sq miles): 353,841
Size (sq km):   916,445

The Lightning Capital of the World: Venezuela is home to Lake Maracaibo, the lightning capital of the world. Here, you can witness the Catatumbo lightning, where storms light up the sky almost nightly. It's like nature's own disco, with lightning bolts instead of disco balls!

Beauty Queens Galore: Venezuela takes beauty pageants super seriously. They've won numerous Miss Universe and Miss World titles. So, don't be surprised if your tour guide looks like they could win a crown. It seems like being beautiful is just another day job here!

Arepa: The Ultimate Snack: In Venezuela, arepas are the go-to snack. These cornmeal patties can be stuffed with pretty much anything. It's like a sandwich, but round, corn-based, and way more fun to fill. Imagine a food so versatile, it's perfect for breakfast, lunch, dinner, and every snack in between!

VIETNAM

Southeast Asia
population: 96,500,000
Size (sq miles): 127,882
Size (sq km): 331,212

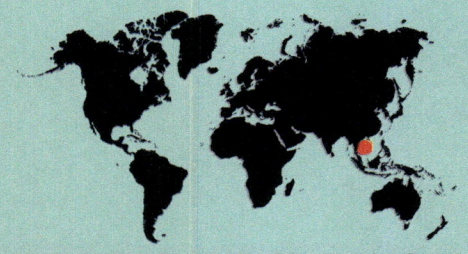

Motorbike Mania: In Vietnam, motorbikes are everywhere! They're like the family car, only cooler and more agile. It's not unusual to see a whole family on one bike, or someone transporting a fridge on the back. Traffic here is like a well-organized chaos on two wheels!

A Wonder Named Ha Long Bay: Imagine 1,600 limestone islands popping out of the sea like giant dragon teeth. That's Ha Long Bay for you, a natural wonder that looks like it came straight out of a fantasy movie. No dragons, though, just stunning scenery!

Coffee with a Twist: Vietnamese coffee isn't just a drink; it's a cultural experience. They love it strong and sweet, often served with condensed milk. And for a real twist, try the egg coffee – yes, it's coffee with a creamy egg topping. It sounds strange but tastes like a liquid tiramisu!

WALES

United Kingdom

Western Europe
population: 3,105,410
Size (sq miles): 8,023
Size (sq km):   20,779

Land of Castles: Wales could be called the castle capital of the world. With over 600 castles, you can't throw a stone without hitting a turret or a drawbridge. It's the perfect place for would-be knights or princesses. Just remember, dragons are harder to find these days!

A Dragon on the Flag: Speaking of dragons, Wales is one of the few countries with a dragon on its flag. This red dragon is not just for show; it's a symbol of Welsh pride and history. It's like having a mythical creature as your personal bodyguard on a flag.

Welsh – A Tongue-Twisting Language: The Welsh language is famous for being a bit of a tongue-twister. With words like "Llanfairpwllgwyngyllgogerychwyrndrobwllllantysiliogogogoch" (yes, it's a real place), you'll need a few practice runs before you say it right. It's like playing a word game every time you read a sign!

WALLIS AND FUTUNA

France

Oceania
population: 11,000
Size (sq miles): 54
Size (sq km): 140

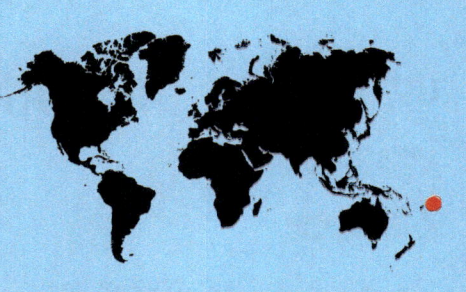

Kingdoms in the Pacific: Wallis and Futuna is unique because it's made up of three traditional kingdoms. Yes, real kingdoms, like in fairy tales, but instead of castles, there are beautiful Pacific island landscapes. It's like having three tiny countries in one, all on islands so small you could almost shout across them! Want more weirdness? It's a part of France!

The Great Pig Mystery: Pigs are highly valued in Wallis and Futuna, almost like family pets – but with a twist. They're often given as gifts for important occasions. So, if you're invited to a big celebration, forget about bringing a bottle of wine; a pig might be more appreciated!

Cricket with a Tropical Spin: Cricket in Wallis and Futuna isn't like the cricket you might know. Here, it's called kilikiti, and it's a more lively and festive version. Picture a cricket match turned into a beach party, with everyone joining in, from kids to grandparents. It's a sport, a party, and a family gathering all in one!

WESTERN SAHARA

Africa
population: 597,000
Size (sq miles): 102,703
Size (sq km): 266,000

The Land of Endless Sand: Western Sahara is dominated by the Sahara Desert, making it one of the most sparsely populated regions on Earth. It's so sandy here, you could play hide and seek with a camel and probably never find it. Just remember, if you're building a sandcastle, you've got plenty of material!

A Coastline with a Secret: The coast of Western Sahara is part of the Canary Current, making it rich in sea life. But here's the twist: it's also known for mysterious shipwrecks. It's like the Bermuda Triangle's less famous cousin, where ships come to play hide and seek with the ocean.

Tea Time, Desert Style: In Western Sahara, making and drinking tea is an art and a way to show hospitality. It's not just a quick cuppa; it's a long, leisurely process with three rounds of tea, each with a different taste. The saying goes, "The first cup is bitter like life, the second is sweet like love, and the third is gentle like death." So, if you're in a rush, maybe stick to water!

YEMEN

Middle East
population: 30,500,000
Size (sq miles): 203,850
Size (sq km): 527,968

Skyscrapers of the Desert: In Yemen, you'll find Shibam, often called 'the Manhattan of the desert'. This ancient city has mud-brick towers up to 11 stories high, built over 500 years ago. It's like a medieval version of New York, but instead of traffic, you have camels strolling by.

A Nation of Chewers: Qat, a plant with mild stimulant properties, is hugely popular in Yemen. In the afternoons, it's common to find people gathering to chew qat leaves and socialize. Think of it as the Yemeni version of a coffee break, just leafier and lasting several hours!

The Dragon's Blood Island: Socotra Island, part of Yemen, is like a piece of another world. It's home to the Dragon's Blood Tree, a bizarrely shaped tree that oozes red sap. This sap was once thought to be dragon's blood (hence the name). The trees look like umbrellas turned inside out, making the landscape feel like a scene from a sci-fi movie.

ZAMBIA

Southern Africa
population: 18,400,000
Size (sq miles): 290,587
Size (sq km):   752,618

The Smoke That Thunders: Zambia is home to Victoria Falls, known locally as Mosi-oa-Tunya, which means "The Smoke That Thunders". This massive waterfall is so huge that its mist can be seen from miles away. It's like the earth decided to go all out with a water show that puts every garden hose to shame.

A Bat Spectacle: Every year, Zambia hosts one of the world's largest mammal migrations, and it's not what you'd expect – it's bats! Millions of fruit bats gather in the Kasanka National Park, creating a sky so full of bats, it could briefly turn day into night. It's like a Batman convention, but with real bats!

Walking on the Wild Side: In Zambia, walking safaris were invented. This is where you can stroll among the wildlife, guided by experts. Imagine taking a walk and saying hi to an elephant or a lion on the way. It's like a hike, but with extra adrenaline and unforgettable selfies!

ZIMBABWE

Southern Africa
population: 14,900,000
Size (sq miles): 150,872
Size (sq km): 390,757

Balancing Rocks: Zimbabwe is famous for its balancing rocks, natural rock formations that look like they're defying gravity. These rocks are so precariously balanced, it seems like they're playing a never-ending game of Jenga with nature. The most famous of these is in Matobo National Park – a true balancing act!

Big, Bigger, Victoria Falls: Sharing Victoria Falls with Zambia, Zimbabwe boasts one of the largest waterfalls in the world. Locals call it 'Mosi-oa-Tunya' or 'The Smoke That Thunders'. The mist and roar can be seen and heard from miles away. It's like nature's own version of a fireworks display, but with water!

A Country Named After a City: Ever heard of the ancient city of Great Zimbabwe? The country is actually named after it! This city, built in the 11th century, was once a bustling metropolis. Today, its impressive stone ruins tell tales of the past. It's like walking into a real-life history book, but with less reading and more exploring.

the world for curious kids

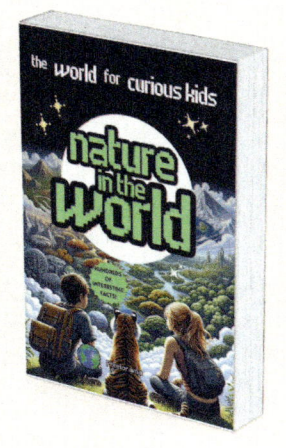

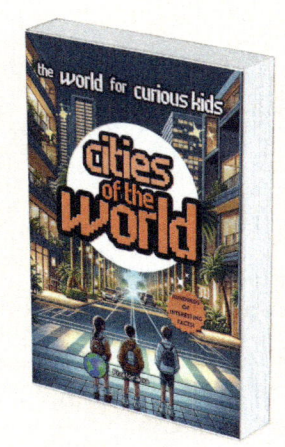

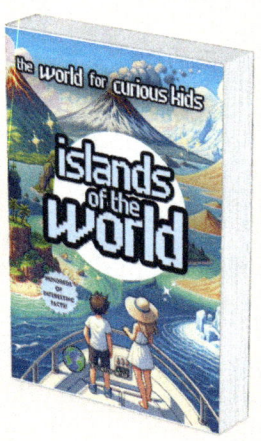

Countries of the World (The World for Curious Kids)
2024 - first edition
© Explorama Books - Pixelorama
exploramabooks@gmail.com

Written and illustrated by: Andrew "PA" Bell, Cameron Wade, Melissa Tusoya, Tajami Hituma, Alex "8-retro", Miguel Alejandro, Nicolas Fontaine, Dorian Reid

All rights reserved. No portion of this book may be reproduced-mechanically, electronically, or by any other means, including photocopying-without written permission of the publisher.

The publisher and authors have done their best to ensure the accuracy and currency of all the information in this book. However, things can change and the publisher and authors can accept no responsibility for any loss, injury, or inconvenience sustained by any traveller as a result of information or advice contained in this book.